# THE INLAND WHALE

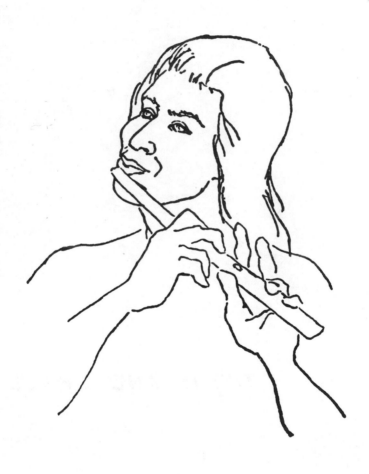

Berkeley, Los Angeles, London

# THE INLAND WHALE

*by Theodora Kroeber*

with a New Foreword by Karl Kroeber

University of California Press

University of California Press, one of the most distinguished university presses in the United States, enriches lives around the world by advancing scholarship in the humanities, social sciences, and natural sciences. Its activities are supported by the UC Press Foundation and by philanthropic contributions from individuals and institutions. For more information, visit www.ucpress.edu.

University of California Press
Berkeley and Los Angeles, California

University of California Press, Ltd.
London, England

Library of Congress Cataloging-in-Publication Data

Kroeber, Theodora.
   The inland whale : nine stories / retold from California
Indian legends by Theodora Kroeber ; with a new foreword by Karl
Kroeber.
      p.      cm.
   Originally published: Bloomington : Indiana University Press, 1959.
   Includes bibliographical references.
   ISBN 0-520-24693-4 (pbk. : alk. paper)
      1. Indians of North America—California—Folklore. I. Title.

E98.F6K76    2006
398.2—dc22                                          2005041873

Manufactured in the United States of America

15   14   13   12   11   10   09   08   07   06
10   9   8   7   6   5   4   3   2   1

This book is printed on New Leaf EcoBook 60, containing 60% post-consumer waste, processed chlorine free; 30% de-inked recycled fiber, elemental chlorine free; and 10% FSC-certified virgin fiber, totally chlorine free. EcoBook 60 is acid-free and meets the minimum requirements of ANSI/ASTM D5634-01 (*Permanence of Paper*).

THIS BOOK *is dedicated to
the ancestors and descendants
of its nine heroines*

# Contents

# Contents

II

# Foreword

WHEN Theodora Kroeber, my mother, translated these stories she was nearing sixty and had never published a book. After her husband, Alfred Kroeber, retired from the Anthropology Department of the University of California, which he had helped to found in 1901, he spent several years as a visiting professor, principally at Columbia, but also at Harvard and later at Chicago and Yale. Then in the early 1950s he and my mother returned to the Maybeck-designed house in Berkeley that they loved.

My father, among other enterprises, set to organizing the huge quantity of ethnographic information on California Indians he had been collecting since the first years of the century, including the recordings of many stories, which had always been of special interest to my mother. For her part, now free from responsibilities to her children, married and scattered about the country, she first made herself into a superb cook (indulging what she called her "champagne tastes") and an elegant gardener, and then began to experiment with writing. She tried children's stories, a genre she never entirely abandoned and in which she later produced one jewel of a book, *A Green Christmas*. Although fond of children and skillful at entertaining them (as her children and grandchildren can testify), what fascinated her most were the complexities of adult psychology.

In 1953 and again in 1954 she and my father drove from Berkeley to the Mojave Indian reservation on the Colorado River. He wanted to verify the accuracy of the detailed geographical references that saturate Mojave myths, which he'd begun recording fifty years earlier. Although he was nearing eighty, he and my mother rented a little boat they rowed and punted up and down the river, identifying sites referenced in the myths. Finally they visited Ha'avulypo in the Black Canyon, where the Mojave god Matavilya had transformed himself into a column of red stone to be an everlasting guardian of the great river his son had created. In those trips originated the idea of *The Inland Whale*. Its next-to-last story—"Tesilya, Sun's Daughter"—my mother created by teasing out from "Cane," a wonderfully elaborate Mojave myth-epic, the embedded history of the hero's faithful wife, Tesilya, patient daughter of the sun.

My mother composed most of the book during the academic year 1956–57, which she and my father spent at the Behavioral Institute at Stanford. There she was encouraged in her project by the psychoanalyst Frieda Fromm-Reichman, with whom my parents became intimate friends. And when the semiologist Thomas Sebeok learned what my mother was writing, he offered to present the completed collection to Bernard Perry, then director of the Indiana University Press. Perry was delighted with the manuscript and immediately recruited a young artist, Joseph Crivy, to illustrate it. Crivy knew absolutely nothing about Indians, and wisely chose to contribute line drawings simply evocative of the delicate sensuality of several of the stories' heroines.

Why did my mother recast these Native American stories instead of making literal translations? She had listened to Indians telling stories, and had shared in my father's study of a vast spectrum of Native American myths from across North America, so she understood why Indian narratives bewilder modern readers unfamiliar with the art of oral storytelling and ignorant of the social circumstances that determine the characters' behavior. In her retellings, she attempted a maneuver similar to that of the distinguished Blackfoot novelist James Welch. To critics who complained that the protagonist of his *Death of Jim Loney* was not obviously Native American in appearance or behavior, Welch explained that he wanted his novel to be read by white people, like the tourists driving along Highway 2 who never saw his native Montana landscape as its native inhabitants did and understood nothing about indigenous "Montana prairie life." Welch said he wanted to "ambush" white readers by luring them into a story that did not seem alien but would gradually lead them to recognize some unfamiliar truths about Native Americans' experience. My mother wished to lure a modern audience into experiencing Indian lifeways as the Indians had, as "normal," not exotic, mysterious, picturesque, or quaint. Only if white readers were made comfortable with the manners, customs, and patterns of behavior familiar to Indian storytellers and listeners could they understand the nuances of emotion and the subtleties of moral purpose which made these stories precious to their original audiences. In this fashion my mother hoped to create appreciation for the exquisite literary art by which Native Californian storytellers had celebrated their centuries-old cultures.

This is why, for example, she constructed her "Loon Woman" story out of versions recorded among eight contiguous Northern California tribal peoples. She wished to distill from these varied but interrelated tellings the Indians' special insight into the tragic consequences of incestuous passions. She sought to recover for contemporary readers the moral tensions such impulses introduce into small, tight-knit, family-based communities which successfully endure by flexibly accommodating quirky individuals, tolerating even radical personal idiosyncrasies, but simultaneously protecting themselves against the social destructiveness of extreme sexual deviancies.

This purpose required my mother to assist readers in imagining Native Californians' "habitus," as sociologist Pierre Bordieu calls the cultural patterning of customary behavior by which the commonest interpersonal relations in daily life are regularly enacted. Unless readers are sensitized to this taken-for-granted canonical behavior and thought, they cannot enter into the meaning for Indians of the unusual events these stories tell. Given today's noisy lifestyle of frenetic consumerism, computer gaming, and restless, guided tourism, nothing is more foreign than the settled, quiet communities Native Californians constructed around intense familial relations and continuous direct interactions with the natural world. Attention to the experiences of women seemed to my mother the best means for imagining our way inside so alien a manner of living. Women engage in the most commonplace and repeated practices of ordinary life and understand the processes upon which these practices depend. We contemporary Western readers may recognize a bow and arrow or bone needle when we see one, but we have never made a bow, an arrow, or a needle. More important, we have never made the stone knife by which such hunting and sewing implements were formed. We have never eaten acorn mush, nor ground the acorns and cooked them in a basket we ourselves wove, filled with stones we heated, carefully not burning our fingers. The evocative, rhythmic narratives of women, women with the creative talent to make customary activities of daily life appear "natural" and for that reason neither unimportant nor uninteresting, my mother thought might best convey the special qualities of Native Californian storytelling.

The "Inland Whale" story evokes the ingrained responsibility felt by each Yurok to sustain the exact coincidence of carefully articulated Yurok culture with the sharply defined coherence of the Yurok natural world. That small world, its continuous vitality embodied in and oriented by the river forever flowing out to meet the encircling sea, contained everything needed for a complex life fulfilling in every way, from the sensual to the spiritual. The holistic religiosity penetrating every aspect of Yurok behavior and thinking endows the displaced whale's magical power with a reality starkly in contrast to the childish wand-waving of our commercialized fantasies. The Yurok whale is a specific manifestation of the power of the world as a whole that unites the livingness of all things—stones, water, plants, animals, humans—a power that enables all things to contribute, each in a unique fashion, to its system of dynamic interdependencies. For humans this requires attaining a balance of mind through spiritual and physical self-purifying in a sweat house, participation in the rituals of communal dancing, and daily adhering to rules of decorous behavior that embody one's commitment to the health of the community. So even a seismic shift of the physical world (California has always been a land of earthquakes) may bring a displaced mother whale where she may gently help a woman loving and loyal to worthy individuals and her son made a bastard by his grandfather's pride. In time, balance is restored through the grandfather's father's exquisite skill in both family relations and profitable craftsmanship, so that the great-grandson can re-legitimate his mother's lineage when it welcomes him to lead the family. The slow, enduring magic of the inland whale is that her restoration of familial-communal order is enacted through reaffirming the preciousness of personal affections. The mother, Nenem, lives out her life back in the family home, but chooses to be buried alongside her lover's humble mother, and persists in her son's memory through her tender smile and the rustle of her dress.

This tale had special resonances for my mother. Nenem's mother-in-law, Huné, could not but have recalled to her Lena Brown, the widowed mother of Theodora's young first husband, who died suddenly, leaving her with two small children. Lena not only took my mother into her house but also made it possible for her to begin graduate study in anthropology. After Theodora's marriage to Alfred Kroeber, Lena remained a staunch friend to the new family (and a tireless reader to a sickly little boy). And when a dozen years after writing this story my mother married for a third time, now to a twenty-nine-year-old artist, her private nickname for him was Toàn.

"Umai" too is a story saturated with assumptions peculiar to the Yurok, yet it pivots on a natural phenomenon that triggered other stories told by different Native Northern Californians, the Modoc, Wintu, and Hupa. The differences between these stories are discussed by my mother in an ethnographic essay in which she describes how the brilliant "fingernail streak" of horizontal light that flashes momentarily just after the sun has set brings together, in all these tellings, a pervasive feeling tone of youthful loneliness made more hauntingly beautiful by evocations of an early, still-empty earth. In a Hupa version, where the story is the central myth of a coming-of-age ceremony, a wonderful image dramatizes the temporality which is the focus of the story: an adolescent girl faces east, against the direction of the river's flow, looking into a polished abalone shell to see the reflected sunset and the horizontal flash of light. "Umai," about two girls literally a world apart who briefly meet and quickly part, is a simpler story whose "effortless form" opens the way for us sympathetically to experience the interpenetration of cosmology and psychology in Yurok imagining that years of ethnological study might not achieve.

Something of the same emotional sensitivity inflects the imaginative nuancing of the Karok love story "About-the-House Girl," with its easy blending of natural and supernatural realms, which no Native American people separated as does the Judeo-Christian tradition. In its interweaving of the imagery of seeing and hearing, of the beauty of Patapir's music drifting along the wind and the shadowed beauty of Ifapi's hidden and partly revealed body, the story evokes the oldest thing in the world, the shy eagerness of first love, that renewed promise of the continuing interdependence of human culture with what is natural.

It is worth remembering that these thoughtful translations open to contemporary imagining ways of life nearly as unfamiliar to other Indians as to white readers, for the independent integrity of each of the California native cultures means that even a Karok probably knew or knows as little of specific Mojave ways as a Yokuts knows of the Yana. It is her sense for such particularity that makes my mother suggest that the story of the butterfly man may have originated in the daydreams of a Wintu woman, much of whose life was spent gathering food and materials for clothing and

[ xvi ]

basketry, trudging with a baby strapped to her back over windswept hills and through the sun-drenched silence of empty valleys. The suggestion points up my mother's sense that women's experience, sometimes slighted even by female ethnographers, offers the deepest if often the most elusive insight into the texture of everyday living of Native Californians. My mother cared nothing for feminist orthodoxy— neither of my parents were sympathetic to any orthodoxy. It was facts, neither fantasies nor ideologies, that fired her imagination, particularly the emotional facts of human relationships, actualized or only desired. By translating a story imaginatively constructed out the commonplaces of a Wintu mother's ordinary life so as to evoke its peculiar responsibilities and lonelinesses, my mother hoped to recover for her readers, from within ancient but disregarded cultures, insight into the haunting pleasures and poignant yearnings that bind men and women together through our very diversity as imaginative beings.

To me she seems to have succeeded beautifully, although I am certainly prejudiced, for I cannot re-read these stories without having come into my memory "her tender smile and the shu-shu-shu-shu rustle of her step, soft and passing as a river breeze."

KARL KROEBER
New York City
July 2005

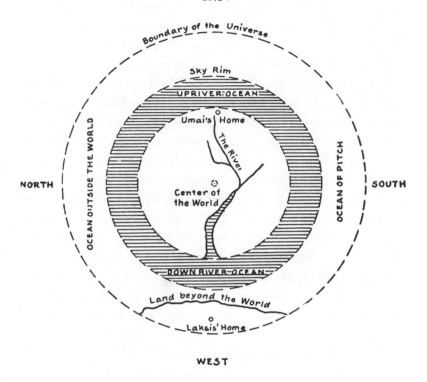

EAST

Boundary of the Universe

Sky Rim

UPRIVER-OCEAN

Umai's Home

The River

NORTH

OCEAN OUTSIDE THE WORLD

Center of the World

OCEAN OF PITCH

SOUTH

DOWN RIVER-OCEAN

Land beyond the World

Laksis' Home

WEST

ANCIENT YUROK WORLD

# Introduction

THIS is a selection of stories from the native Indian literature of California, made for the adult reader who has a general interest in comparative literature, but not in technical folklore or linguistics as such.

The stories are authentic. A list of their sources will be found at the end of the book. The plots and persons are the stories' own, but in my retelling the focus of interest changes, almost imperceptibly in some, sharply in others. All carrying over of an art, whether it is plastic, musical, or literary, from another age and culture and language into our own brings with it some change of focus. We associate the texture and whiteness of marble with classical Greek sculpture, whereas the Athenians of Praxiteles' day were accustomed to a vivid and multicolor painted sculpture. We hear an Arcadian wistfulness and a whispering delicacy in "baroque" music, which to its own age was passionate and full-bodied. And so it is with literature. We are less interested in the routes they traversed and in the exploits of their heroes than were the Indians, and more interested in the character and personality of the hero or his wife or an old uncle. A work of art has more facets than are turned to the light at one time.

My objective has been to transmit in some measure the sense of poetry and drama which these tales held for their own people. This has meant leaving out episodes which are intractable to transmutation or which were present in the original because the storyteller and his audience were not averse to borrowing episodes from other stories; and it has meant making explicit many things which the native listener would not need to have included, because they would be commonplaces to him. The alien reader must be given enough background fact so that motivation and behavior are understood. He may need to know something as simple as the floor plan of a house, or the native concept of geography or etiquette or belief.

In the latter part of the book there is some general discussion of the place of an oral literature within the family of comparative literature, followed by a review of the literary and the human aspects of the stories, comparing them one with another and with the categories of modern Western literature.

Within each tale is a portrait of a woman, some scarcely

more than a shadowed outline, some fully revealed. It seemed best to have a unifying *locus* since the possible choice is various and wide, and a heroine is a heroine, young, beautiful, or old, or evil, whether she is Indian or English. I have tried not to revalue, not to judge the women whose stories I tell, but to bring them to you, to whom they are strange, as they were seen by their peers. Some stories I started, and then regretfully dropped, unsure of their cadence and feeling tone. I am conscious of a staticness, an absence of the visual as such, a quality as of the archaic smile in all my women. It is as much as I am sure I see.

THEODORA KROEBER

*The Inland Whale*

THE house Pekwoi is in the village of Kotep, close to the Center of the World. It is the custom among the River People for the wealthy and aristocratic to give names to their houses, and such a house is Pekwoi.

The pattern of Kotep, which is in the canyon, is that its named houses are built in rows high above the river, with sun and view. Below them, the rows begin to straggle and only an occasional house will have a name. And at the sunless bottom of the canyon cluster the mean and ramshackle and nameless houses of the poor.

Pekwoi's sunny terrace of matched stone looks upriver as far as the bend and downriver as far as eye can see. Its round doorframe is carefully carved; the redwood planks of its walls and roof bear marks of the finest adzing. Inside, it is dry against the rains, tight against the winds.

Long, long ago, for Pekwoi is old, a fire burned night and day in the pit. Around the four sides on the main floor and on the shelves under the eaves were stored the long boxes filled with treasure and the great baskets filled with the fruits of ocean, river, bush, and tree, fresh and dried. In the pit close to the fire lay the deerskin blankets for sitting comfortably or for sleeping warmly.

Such was Pekwoi in the time when Nenem and Nenem's father and mother and grandparents lived there. Nenem and her proud and aristocratic family were known and respected all up and down the river. No Jumping Dance took place in Nenem's time without the wolfskin headbands and the civet aprons from Pekwoi; no Deerskin Dance was complete without the priceless pure white deerskin of Pekwoi.

Nenem herself had a tender rhythmic sort of beauty. Her heavy hair, parted in the middle and held with mink-skin ties, lay straight and shining over her shoulders and breasts. Ear disks of polished abalone shell framed a gentle face, high-bred in its modeling, with long eyes and crescent-moon eyebrows and a gracious mouth. She was small and she moved with a light proud step, so smoothly that the many-stranded shell beads around her neck and the hundreds of strings of seeds in her apron and the heavy polished abalone and obsidian pendants which hung from her buckskin skirt made only a soft shu-shu-shu-shu accompaniment to her walk.

Her father expected to receive the highest bride price for Nenem when she should choose to marry, and he expected her choice to be made from among the most eligible. It came out quite otherwise, however. Nenem fell in love with a young man there in the village, the son of a widowed and impoverished mother, obscure and without family. He and his mother lived in one of the most primitive of the shacks along the river's edge. They were so poor and so little known that at this distance of time not even the name of the young man is preserved to us.

Nenem's nameless lover must, nonetheless, have been a person of some positive attributes of person and character for Nenem truly and wholly loved him. When she knew that she was to have a child by him, he and she went to her family and told them and said they wished to be man and wife. Nenem's parents and family were shocked and outraged. Her lover could not pay a bride price that would have been other than insulting to this family.

He knew this and he said to Nenem's father, "It is my wish to be full-married to your daughter; to earn her and to deserve her. I will, if you will have it so, work faithfully for you and do whatever you order me to do and be a good son to you. If you will not have it so—here I am— kill me. This is your right." But the father was too proud to kill one whom he considered so far beneath him. "Then take me as your slave—do with me what you will," he said.

But it was intolerable to the father to so much as look

at his daughter's lover. He could not bear to have him at Pekwoi or even in Kotep.

Nenem, in deep disgrace, was not allowed to leave Pekwoi. Her lover, without money or powerful friends, was quite helpless. In despair, he left the village and was lost to Nenem and to his mother. Neither they nor anyone ever heard of him again. It is believed in Kotep that he was murdered in the lonely hills beyond the river.

Her parents' fury turned full on Nenem as soon as her lover was gone from Kotep. In their hurt pride and the disappointment of all their hopes for her, they drove her out of Pekwoi and declared her to be no longer their daughter.

What the distracted Nenem might have done, one can only imagine. Before there was time for her to make any of the desperate decisions of the disgraced and abandoned, the mother of her lover, the old woman Hunè, took her home to the shabby dwelling by the river's edge where she and her son had always lived. There she cared for Nenem and comforted her and loved her as her own daughter. And in the same humble house, Nenem bore a son after some moons, and Hunè was mother and midwife and nurse to her. And not even in Pekwoi would the elaborate ritual of the birth and first moon of a son have been more rigidly enacted than it was in this same house.

Nenem called the baby Toàn. He was a strong, happy baby. Hunè cared for him and his mother, and she had the joy of recognizing his first words and of watching him learn to take his first steps on his short sturdy legs. The moons waxed and waned and the seasons were new and grew old and went and came again. Toàn lost his first roundness and the sturdy legs grew longer and carried him, running, tireless, at her side.

The river gave them salmon to eat fresh and to smoke and dry. Hunè's storage baskets bulged with fat acorns gathered from the oak trees that the people of Kotep harvest. Hunè and Nenem searched the sunny hillsides of late spring and early summer for the grasses with which to weave hats and cooking and serving baskets, and they picked up any pieces of pine root they found for repairing the heavy old storage baskets. They kept themselves decently and cleanly dressed in fresh bark skirts and aprons. They set snares for rabbits and they were warm in winter under rabbit-skin blankets.

With no man to care for it, Hunè's house was becoming little more than a patchwork of old planks somehow renewed when she and Nenem found a discarded board along the river or when a canoe broke up and they were able to salvage parts of it for a new door ledge or other replacement. The noonday sun shone through holes in the roof now.

Hunè lived for one more World Renewal ceremony and then before spring came, she died. This was a heavy grief and loneliness to Nenem, and as long as she lived she missed Hunè and cried in loving memory of her.

The summer after Hunè's death came and went without event and it was time for the World Renewal ceremony again. The dancing was to be upriver from Kotep this year and almost everyone in Kotep was already on his way there, either by canoe or trail. Only Nenem and Toàn remained at home. Nenem was leaching acorns by the river, when several canoes filled with people from down-river came by and the people recognized her. Their voices carried to her across the water, "Nenem! Nenem! Come along with us—we've plenty of room!"

"Oh—thank you—thank you!—I can't go—I'm not ready —I—" Nenem's answering call showed her reluctance.

One of them who knew her well, called out coaxingly, "Nenem! Surely you are not staying away from the danc-ing!"

Nenem hesitated to admit that indeed she had meant not to go at all. Instead, she answered, "I'll be a little late. You mustn't wait—I'm coming—I'll be there in time for the Ending Dances!"

Her friends in the canoes went on since she seemed really to wish it so. When they were gone, Nenem, having said she was coming, did get herself and Toàn ready and, taking some food and such other things as they might need, she set off by foot trail upriver.

She reached the dancing place in time for the Ending Dances as she had said she would. Everyone was there. It was evening and the fire illumined the faces of the danc-ers and of the onlookers equally. There were four dance teams. One of them was dancing and the other three were standing in formal lines, waiting their turn.

The onlookers were arranged with equal formality. Closest to the dancers on the right side sat the men of the great families of the river; and on the left side, the women of these families. The common people stood behind, but separated in the same manner—the men on the right and the women on the left. Nenem joined the group of standing women. She was gentle-mannered and gracious as always and thanks to Huné's example, she and her small son were as carefully groomed and dressed as though they had been carried by canoe straight from Pekwoi itself.

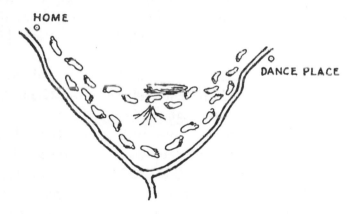

There was a slight rustle as the women in the front row moved over so that Nenem might join them there. They motioned to her to come up with them and one of them took her arm and guided her to her seat and made her sit among them. They all greeted her, and between the dances they showed her the customary courtesies of friendliness and the special and formal ones due the honored daughter of a first family.

[ 13 ]

Nenem's own blood relatives ignored her—her coming —her son—her being seated.

Nenem did not know how to refuse the kindnesses and courtesies shown her by everyone except her family. She was already upset and when she saw the white deerskin of Pekwoi on its pole in the dance, she could not bear to sit there, so close, and in her old natural place. She slipped quietly away, little Toàn asleep in her arms. It did not occur to her friends that she was leaving for more than the moment. No one saw her start back down the trail toward Kotep, carrying Toàn and crying bitterly, bitterly.

Nenem kept to the river trail as far as Atsìpul Creek where there is a fork. Here she left the river, taking the fork which leads back through the hills and around Kewet Mountain and rejoins the river trail only a little above Kotep. This is a rough and steep way to go. Nenem chose it because it is not much used and it would bring her home without going through any of the larger villages along the river. In her present unhappy state she dreaded meeting anyone.

Toàn wakened and wondered much at his mother's tears, for she continued to cry. It was a clear night with a moon. Nenem put Toàn down and let him walk and the two of them wandered on up through the hills as far as a small mountain lake called Fish Lake. By this time Nenem was quite worn out and she made camp. They slept there the rest of the night by the lake.

To a world in balance, the flat earth's rise and fall, as it floats on Underneath Ocean, is almost imperceptible, and nothing is disturbed by it. Doctors know that to keep this balance, the people must dance the World Renewal dances, bringing their feet down strong and hard on the earth. If they are careless about this, it tips up and if it tips more than a very little, there are strange and terrible misplacements. One of the worst of these occurred before Nenem's grandparents' time and her unhappy father traced his own troubles to it. Most people along the river would agree with him.

This was the time when the earth tipped so far that Downriver Ocean came over the bar and flowed up the river, filling and overflowing the canyon, carrying its waters and its fish and other sea life far inland, past even the Center of the World—farther than it had ever penetrated before. With prayers and dancing, balance was eventually restored and the ocean flowed back down the canyon and outside the bar, carrying the fish and other sea life with it, except for a young female whale who had been washed all the way into Fish Lake and was left stranded there.

Ninawa, the whale, had lain there all this while, scarcely able to move, for she reached almost from one side of the lake to the other; and when she slapped her tail as whales do, she threw mud as far as the encircling meadow.

She was quiet the night Nenem and Toàn slept beside her. She listened to Nenem's crying in the night and in the morning, for Nenem's tears started again as soon as she wakened.) And she heard what Nenem said through her tears. Then Ninawa knew why Nenem cried and she was glad that the ocean had brought her and left her stranded here. For Ninawa was no ordinary whale. These things about her were special: she had great power; she was compassionate to all suffering but particularly to Nenem's suffering. And this was because Ninawa was a bastard like Toàn.

Ninawa dared not move, lest she frighten Nenem and Toàn, and she had determined to help them. She lay still, making herself look as much as possible like a log fallen across the lake, and thinking and willing one thing all of the time: that Toàn should sit on her or climb on her; that he should somehow come and touch her if only for a moment, so that some of her power might flow into him.

Nenem would have followed the Kewet trail around the lake when she was ready to leave in the morning, except that Toàn distracted her from doing so. He had been playing at the water's edge all morning, and now he went a little farther and a little farther, until he was wading in water quite deep for him. And there beside him was Ninawa—something solid and rough and most tempting to climb. Toàn climbed; and when Nenem looked around for him, he was on top of what she, through her tears, took to be an enormous old water-soaked log, lying like a bridge across the lake.

Nenem was frightened, realizing how easily Toàn might slip or stumble. She had the wisdom not to cry out or startle him. She merely waded out as he had done and climbed up on Ninawa, following after him as fast as she could go. She knew that if anything were to happen to Toàn, she had no wish to live. But nothing happened to Toàn. He ran along ahead of her, on Ninawa's broad back, and when they came to the other end of their "log," they climbed down, waded to shore and went on their way to Kewet Mountain.

Ninawa shook ever so slightly when Toàn first touched her and she trembled as he left her. Toàn would recall this many moons from now, but he and his mother did not think much about it at the time.

Nenem had never been inland before. It was a long day's walk for her, carrying Toàn much of the time, around Kewet Mountain. She was relieved when the trail finally came back to the river and she knew she had not lost her way.

It was after dark when she and Toàn reached home. They ate a cold supper and went to bed without lighting a fire. As soon as her neighbors saw the smoke from her morning fire, they came to make sure she and Toàn had come to no harm. After all, no one had seen them, either at Kotep or at any of the villages along the river for two nights, and they were fearful for them. They did not press Nenem to talk—they saw her tears were yet too close. But her sore heart was eased; she knew she had come home to friends.

Nenem and Toàn had another friend—Nenem's father's father, Toàn's great-grandfather. It is not the way of the aged, if they are wise, to raise their voices against the decisions and actions of the household. And this great-grandfather was wise. He watched Nenem and Toàn and waited.

The day came when great-grandfather took his tools and the wood he was carving and sat down close to Hunè's house where Toàn was playing. Toàn, full of interest and curiosity, came and sat beside him and watched him carve. Great-grandfather appeared to be making a boat. He explained that it was not to be a boat, however, but a box; a hollowed-out box with a cover that would lash on and close tight. Toàn wanted to make a hollowed-out box, too. With great-grandfather's help, he gouged and cut and whittled until, by the end of the afternoon, Toàn's box was finished. It was a very small box, but it was complete with its own small lid and lashings. (Great-grandfather had contributed a piece of moccasin lace.)

Great-grandfather suggested that, having a box, he might collect pretty bird feathers and store them in his box. Toàn collected fallen feathers and soon the box was full and he and great-grandfather carved out a bigger box. To fill this one, they no longer contented themselves with collecting feathers. Great-grandfather made bow and arrows and brought light sharp arrow points from his store of them. Then he taught Toàn to shoot and to hunt.

As Toàn grew older and went hunting alone or with other boys, he continued to bring to his great-grandfather little birds, then bigger birds, and especially the red-headed woodpecker, and then the fur animals—whatever he could hunt or trap. Together, they cleaned the feathers and scraped the skins and stored them away in their boxes. As they needed them, they made more boxes, always bigger and handsomer ones, and these, too, began to be filled with treasure.

Toàn sometimes hunted inland on Kewet Mountain and as far as Fish Lake. Whenever he was at the lake, he wondered what had become of the log on which he had climbed that first time, with his mother, for it was no longer there. He recalled how it had trembled under his touch and he thought again of how his mother had cried. He had not known there were such tears in the world until that day.

All this great-grandfather did for Toàn without once raising his voice against his son or his daughter-in-law in Pekwoi.

Great-grandfather died as Toàn was coming to his first manhood. He left a great-grandson looking forward to a different sort of world from that Nenem had feared he would be facing. For there in Hunè's house were many, many boxes, carved by a sure young hand and filled with the prowess of a remarkably skilled young hunter.

Great-grandfather was dead. There was the funeral and there was the mourning. Toàn went to Fish Lake alone, for he was bereft and grieved by this death. He lay down by the lake and went to sleep. As he slept, he dreamed.

Ninawa came to him in his dream, and she told him many things. She told him that she, Ninawa, was the In-

land Whale; that she was the "log" on which he and his
mother had crossed Fish Lake; and that, after they were
gone, the Inland Spirits came and carried her to another
lake. She did not tell him where the lake is, for it is not
given to anyone but an occasional Doctor in trance or,
briefly, to a specially purified person, to see or know this
lake. Ninawa said of it only that it is far, far inland, that it
is big enough for a whale to live in comfortably and to
slap her tail without striking mud, that it is boat-shaped
and ringed round with oak trees.

In the dream, Ninawa slapped her tail as whales do,
and spoke. "Toàn," she said, "Toàn, you should know that
the winter moons are children of no-marriages—bastards
like you and me. I listened to your mother crying over you
for a night and a day, when you were too young to know
why she cried, and I pitied you.

"Then I remembered—it is the bastard winter moons
that bring the rains and the strength to the Earth for the
budding and blooming and gathering of the full-marriage
moons of spring and summer and autumn. And I determined that you, too, should have the strength of a winter moon, and I willed you to come to me. You came to
me, and when you touched me, I trembled. Do you remember, Toàn? That was because I so much wanted you
to come and dreaded lest I with my great size might
frighten you away. But you had no fear and you climbed
up and walked on my back. Do you remember that, Toàn?
Here in Fish Lake it was. You walked from my tail to my

head, and while you walked, I made my power flow through you.

"You will go on as you are. You will be a good man as you are a good boy; you will be a great hunter; you will own much treasure and wealth, and you will be remembered as the greatest of the sons of Pekwoi.

"Remember all that great-grandfather taught you. Cry also to the bastard winter moons when you pray. And never forget that once you walked on Ninawa's back." This is what Ninawa said to Toàn.

When Toàn wakened, hours later, Ninawa was not there. He lay still, recalling her words, memorizing them so that as long as he lived, he remembered them.

Nenem taught Toàn the words and gestures of greetings and of leave-takings, the ways of holding the elk-horn spoon and the basket when eating, what to do with the hands and the arms and the body, how to speak and to modulate the voice, the rules of precedence—the whole complicated etiquette of the aristocrat. He learned from her example the courtesy and graciousness and openness of the well-born.

One thing more Nenem taught Toàn before he was big enough to go to the sweat house: the severe and rigid code of a proud house. Toàn learned earlier than do most boys to fast and to purify himself and to practice control so that pain, anger, greed, excessive feeling of any sort did not show in his expression or in his actions.

By the time he went from Nenem's instruction to that of the sweat house, he was well accustomed to discipline and restraint. And once he went to the sweat house, he followed its pattern of behavior. He went far off to gather wood for the ceremonies there; he prayed long and exhausting hours at the shrines in the hills; he adhered to the rules of fasting, chastity, and purification imposed on the hunter. When he fasted and prayed, he cried out to his great-grandfather and to the bastard winter moons as Ninawa had said to do, and through it all, Toàn never forgot that once he had walked on Ninawa's back.

Five times the moons of the winter rains gave way to the moons of the first green buds. Nenem looked at her son. She saw that he was a proud and brave and good man as Ninawa had said he would be, and Nenem was satisfied.

Toàn was scarcely full grown when his bulging boxes could outfit a Deerskin Dance upriver and a Jumping Dance downriver at the same time. Such an accumulation of treasure by one so young had not happened before on the river and perhaps has not happened since. And it was the more remarkable, since the power and wealth and prestige of Pekwoi were denied him. Ninawa had supplied, in her own way, more even than Pekwoi withheld.

Ninawa's power sent his arrows farther and straighter, but the tireless hunter was Toàn. From hummingbird to blackbird to woodpecker to eagle to condor; from weasel to mink to civet cat to wolf to deer—Toàn snared and netted and trapped and decoyed and hunted. He cleaned and tanned and glued and cut and sewed as great-grand-father and his mother had taught him to do.

It was Ninawa's power that spread the word of this hunter who might sell or trade his surplus. She started the flow of those with money for purchasing and those with sea lion tusks and rare obsidian and flint, who sought him out. But the buyers and traders came again and again because they were pleased with him and with what he offered. Trading and selling far upriver and downriver to the sea, Toàn gradually filled a large box with the precious long strings of dentalium shell money.

At last Toàn could afford to hire the skilled old crafts-men of Kotep to work moon after moon after moon, mak-ing up his feathers and furs and skins and ivories and flints and obsidians into treasure of incredible beauty and value. And Toàn was free to go farther and farther afield, searching out the rare, the unique, and the beautiful, in bird and animal and rock and shell.

Meanwhile Pekwoi stood—a proud house—whose pres-ent occupants fed their pride on its past.

Nenem's father died, the last of the older generations.

Then the younger men of Pekwoi, Nenem's brother and his two sons, came with all of the principal men of Kotep, to Hunè's house. The brother was their spokesman; in their name and his own, he invited Toàn to live in Pekwoi and to be the head of the house. When he was finished speaking, the others urged Toàn to accept his uncle's invitation.

Toàn turned to his mother. "What should I do, mother? What do you want me to do?" he asked her.

"You should go, Toàn. I wish you to go," was what Nenem answered.

That is how it was that Toàn came home to Pekwoi, and the people of Kotep and of the other villages felt this to be a right and good thing. And far away in a boat-shaped lake ringed round with oak trees, a bastard female whale trembled and slapped her tail as whales do. And Nenem gazed up the steep canyon side to where Pekwoi stood, its round carved door open to the sun, and she smiled from a serene and grateful heart; then Nenem turned and went inside Hunè's house.

The boxes and treasure and money went with Toàn to Pekwoi. But Nenem did not go. Her brother invited her and everyone at Pekwoi wanted and expected her and Toàn urged her almost frantically. It was no use. Toàn had to leave her where she was.

She told him, "You must go. What would you do here— how could you live here? It is no sort of place for the First Man of the village and the family you will have one day soon. But this is my home and I have no wish to live anywhere else—ever."

So Nenem lived on in the house which had sheltered her and her baby. Its shabby walls, its old baskets and keepsakes were home to her, her near neighbors were her dear friends. Toàn understood this but he was never wholly reconciled to her staying there, and he asked her over and over to come to Pekwoi; and when Toàn bought himself a wife from one of the great houses of Olegel, upriver, his wife too urged her mother-in-law to come to them, and after a while there were grandchildren, and they asked her to come.

She always answered the same way, "Some day, some day," putting them off.

She protested when Toàn wanted to give her house a solid roof. She loved the briar and manroot vines which had grown up the sides of the house and over the roof, filtering the noon sun which shone in briefly through the holes and screening them from the rain. She and her friends called the house "Briar Roof" and she would say coaxingly to Toàn, "Don't you see? I too live in a named house now!"

Toàn did as much as his mother would let him do to make the house more habitable for one no longer young, and to keep it in some sort of repair. But after many winter moons had shone on "Briar Roof," he said firmly she must come to them before another season of storms, else he must certainly build her a new house on the site of Hunè's old one.

Nenem did not want that. She said, "No! I will come to your house—to Pekwoi—with you."

So, at last, Nenem, too, came home to Pekwoi.

Nenem fitted Pekwoi and completed it. She was the grandmother it had been missing. Toàn saw how his children liked to be near her. He watched her going up and down the little ladder to the pit and in and out of the low round door, her step smooth and light as always. He liked best to find her sitting, feet tucked under, on the sunny terrace, working at one of her perfect basketry pieces. Then he would sit on a redwood block, close by, carving or watching her. He would have been at peace then—there really was nothing more he desired—except that he sensed something not wholly right in his mother.

One day, they were sitting so and Toàn said to her, "What is it that troubles you, my mother? Can you tell me?"

In her usual, quiet voice Nenem tried to tell him, "It is that I know I won't live much longer, and . . . and . . ."

But Toàn, dreading lest his mother see that in his heart he knew this to be true, interrupted her, speaking as lightly as he could, "You must wait awhile till I kill a very special deer so you can have the most beautiful skirt in the world to wear when you die . . . would you like that?"

Nenem reached over and put her arms around him. "No . . . no . . . Toàn . . . that is what I've been wanting to tell you . . . in my grave I wish to wear a maple bark skirt and apron like the ones your father's mother always wore—nothing else. Will you dress me so when I die?"

"If that is what you wish . . ."

"And . . . one thing more . . . I want to be buried beside her. Will you do that, Toàn?"

"I will bury you beside her," Toàn promised.

"There is nothing else, my son." Nenem smiled her tender smile and Toàn no longer saw the look of trouble in her eyes.

Before the last moon of winter was full, Nenem was dead.

Alone, Toàn observed the full burial ritual. This was his wish. His wife and Nenem's close friends, who helped him dress her and make her ready, took the grapevine cord which was used to lower her into her grave, and passing it slowly down over their bodies, handed it to Toàn, thus passing on to him their contamination from the dead.

Alone, Toàn cried and fasted for five days, speaking to no one, drinking no water, eating only a little thin acorn gruel. Each night, he made a fire on his mother's grave to warm her until she should have had time to make her journey to the land of the dead.

At the end of the five days, he went to the sweat house where an old man of Kotep performed the ceremony of burial purification. He washed Toàn with an infusion of roots and aromatic herbs, meanwhile praying to each of the Inland Spirits who live along the river and blowing a puff of the sacred tobacco smoke from his pipe toward each of them in turn. And so he came finally to the Spirit who lives at the mouth of the river, just inside the bar. The ritual response of this One, after the prayer and the smoke offering, was that the corpse contamination was removed. Toàn's purification was now complete, and he was free to return to his wife in Pekwoi and to go hunting once more.

Toàn had remembered his promise to his mother. He dressed her only in a fresh maple bark skirt and apron and he buried her beside the mother of her lover. Their graves are still there today, at the river's edge, close to a grassy hollow which is all that is left of Hunè's house. Toàn cared for them and kept the tops clean as long as he lived, as did his children and his children's children, after him.

Nenem had taught Toàn, long ago, that it is wrong to grie e too much for the dead, that it is dangerous for those near to you even to think too much about one who has died; and Toàn remembered this teaching. He passed his mother's grave whenever he went to the river, and sometimes he took his carving and sat near where she lay while he worked, as he had sat near her all his life. He cried to her sometimes, but for the most part, her tender smile and the shu-shu-shu-shu rustle of her step came into his memory and out again, soft and passing as a river breeze.

*Loon Woman*

A BACK country, rough and remote, a place of hills and woods, of clear streams and reed-rimmed lakes—this is Loon Woman's country. Except for a few fishermen and hunters who find their way there, and an occasional family which lives in a clearing in the forest, it is as lonely of people now as it was in Loon Woman's time. The villages cluster now, as anciently, alongside the river only after it has reached the rich lowland valley and collected all the little streams to itself and become muddy and broad and slow.

You may sometime be in Loon Woman's country, and you may see this thing which I will tell you of and which repeats itself from time to time. A hunter stands half concealed in the reeds by one of the lakes. Dark wings beat clumsily over his head and a female loon lands on the lake, calling her raucous call. It sounds like crazy laughing mixed with crazy crying, and it reminds the hunter of Ishanihura who lived long, long ago and who came to be the Loon Woman. The hunter watches the loon. She paddles to shore and settles herself on the sand, where she gazes at her own upside-down image in the still lake-mirror. She preens her black-grey feathers and goes into an awkward dance, standing on one foot and shifting stiffly to the other and back again, turning her neck from side to side and pulling her head forward so that the band of white around her throat stands out. To the hunter, the band looks like a string of human hearts, old and shrunken and bleached to whiteness, and he remembers that Ishanihura wore a necklace like this one. Though he makes no sound, the air over the lake becomes alerted. Taking alarm, the loon dives. Too late. The arrow has already pierced the band of white and entered her heart. She goes under and comes up dead. The hunter retrieves his arrow and throws the bird aside where scavenging buzzards promptly find it. All this he does because he hopes thus to keep Ishanihura's ancient evil from his people.

This is Ishanihura's story:

In the beginning, Ishanihura was a young girl like any other. She grew up, one sister among nine brothers, beloved and cared for. The first-born was a son, Makikirèn, a gentle child, and so beautiful that his father and mother sighed when they looked at him; they knew it is hard to guard such beauty. Ishanihura came next, as self-willed and passionate as her elder brother was beautiful. After her came eight more boys, and the earth-covered house in the clearing in the lonely hills was full.

The parents tried to teach their children the way of life: what to believe, what to do, and what not to do. The children knew how the world was created and about the beginnings of things. They learned the People's history, its songs and stories, and they learned the language of women. Ishanihura and her mother spoke only this language, and the father and brothers used it when speaking with them. Ishanihura learned to cook and to gather and store seeds, to make flour, to sew, and to make baskets. From their father the boys learned the language which men use among themselves; and they learned to hunt and trap and fish, to build shelters and houses, and to fashion tools.

It was a good life and it was the way. The father and mother should have been happy; but during the peaceful summers of childhood, their children playing nearby, the parents continued to feel an unease they could not name. Makikirèn grew tall and straight and ever more beautiful, and, because they felt him to be somehow threatened, they were much given to keeping him out of sight and away from the others and to sending him for longer and longer visits to his grandparents downriver. More and more, as he grew up, he travelled by himself, until one day he found his way up to the sky floor, where he made

[ 33 ]

friends with the Sky People. From that day, he spent much of his time there. Perhaps the sky floor was closer to the earth in ancient times than it is now, for we know that the wild geese and other high flying birds flew easily up into the sky world and that there were people like Makikirèn who came and went between earth and sky by way of the sky pole; and all this cannot be so easily done today.

To his sister it seemed that Makikirèn had quite disappeared from home. She questioned her mother about him at first, but with time it came to seem natural for him to be away. She no longer asked where he was.

Ishanihura reached the age of the once-a-moon periods, the age when a girl becomes a woman. She lived alone during her moon periods in a small earth-covered house, built for her alongside the big family house. Never a very happy or sunny child, she was more than ever restless and moody and discontent, and her parents thought that soon, very soon, they must arrange to have her visit the villages in the lowlands where, staying with her grandparents, she could make friends with her cousins and with girls her own age, and meet the young men of the lowlands. A husband would be chosen for her from among these men, sons of her parents' friends. Ishanihura was not much interested in meeting the lowland people, and as yet there were only vague plans with no time fixed for her going.

Behind the earth-covered house and some distance away in the trees there was a spring, and below, a shaded pool fed by the spring. Here Ishanihura and her mother came to fetch water and to wash, and here her father and brothers came naked from the sweat house for their after-sweating plunge. It was a quiet woodland place, and Ishanihura liked to sit by the water looking into its dark depths and dreaming her own strange dark dreams. She was sitting so one day, running her hand idly through the water, when a single long human hair curled along one hand and arm as she raised it from the water. She took an end of the hair and held it out straight, wondering whose it was: not hers or her mother's, because it was too coarse; not her father's, because his was not so long as this one. Since no one but her family swam here, it must belong to one of her brothers.

Which brother?

She measured the hair against her own long hair. They were the same length.

Which brother?

She stroked the hair slowly between her fingers, down its length and down again while the day went from sun to shadow. Her mother called to her, and she wrapped the hair around one of the ties which held her own. As she stood up to go she saw her reflection in the pool, and, watching this dark, distorting image, she danced a strange stiff dance, flapping her arms and turning her head from side to side until her mother called again and Ishanihura ran quickly home.

After the evening meal, Ishanihura's father went to the sweat house for the night, taking the two older boys with

[ 35 ]

him. Makikirèn was never with the family these days. Ishanihura and her mother and the boys left at home sat by the fire for a while, and the children coaxed their mother to tell them a story.

She told them the long story of how the world was made, with valleys and mountains, springs and rivers and lakes, plants and trees, and finally, all the animals. From far above the earth, Eagle, the Creator, looked down upon it and it seemed complete, except that it had no people. Eagle called his two children to him, a son and a daughter, telling them to go down and live on the earth that there might be people there. They went and they were alone on the earth, just the two of them. The boy said to his sister, "Let us sleep together!" She did not answer him. Five times he asked her and after the fifth time, she said, "Why do you ask such a thing? You are my brother." He said, "We are alone. There are no other people. If we sleep together here, there will be children born and we will no longer be alone. That is why our father, Eagle, sent us down here." Then his sister consented and they slept together and created children. When they had done this, Eagle assigned his grandchildren to special places, some to one fold of hills, some to another, and there they lived and became the different people, like people today. A marriage of brother and sister, the mother went on to say, happened only once, only in the very beginning, during the creation.

The children listened to the story, and as they listened Ishanihura stroked and parted and smoothed the hair of

[ 36 ]

her youngest brother. Sitting just outside the circle of firelight, she unwound an end of the hair she had found and rolled it between her fingers. She could feel that it was coarser than this youngest's. She slid along between the next two boys, stroked their hair, parted it and compared it with the hair from the pool. It was coarser than theirs. By this time the older boys were coaxing her to come and smooth their hair, too. She did this and she could tell that theirs was more like the hair from the pool. Secretly, she unwound it and measured its length against theirs, but theirs was shorter by a thumb's length. The hair must belong to one of the boys who was with her father.

She would have to think of some other way to find out which one, now that those two were old enough to sleep in the men's house. She did not see very much of them anymore, and, ever since she had had her separate house, they had been less easy with her. They wouldn't think of asking her to comb their hair now, and her mother would, she knew, disapprove if she offered to.

The next time she went to stay in her house of the moons, she sat alone as the sun went down and the woods grew dusky, dreaming her strange and lonely young girl dreams; and tonight the hair that had clung to her arm from the pool wound and wove through her dreams. To know whose hair it was that she carried wrapped around her own! She heard her father and her older brothers praying and singing in the sweat house. They would, she knew, be going to the pool soon. And as she listened to

[ 37 ]

them, she thought of a way to learn what she so much wanted to know. The night was clear with only the dark illumination of the stars, and Ishanihura slipped out of her house and hid close to the pool.

The sweat house door opened as she expected, but only one person came out. There followed the light sound of bare feet running on the earth and a shadowed figure passed so close she could have touched him. The runner raised his hands straight over his head, the fingers together, spearlike, and Ishanihura watched as he made a running dive, smooth and splashless, almost without sound. He dived and came up and swam the circle of the pool two or three times. Then he pulled himself out onto the bank and sat by the pool's edge, wringing out his long hair and wiping the glistening drops down his arms and body and legs. This done, he went quickly, lightly, back up the hill, disappearing into the shadow, into the night.

When he was gone, Ishanihura crawled cautiously to the edge where he had sat to wring out his hair—cautiously, because the others might follow him. And there, as she had hoped, she found another hair. Still cautious, still crawling, she went back through the dark toward her own little house, this newest hair wound around her neck. Once inside, she stirred up the fire and in the firelight unwound and measured and compared her two hairs from the pool. They were identical. She held them up and watched them as they waved in the air before her eyes, and it came to Ishanihura that she must have the one whose hair was the same length as hers—the swift-moving, shadowed one, the one who swam alone.

She frowned as she sat by the fire.

Which brother?

And why did only one brother come?

Well, she would soon discover which. She need only be careful and watchful a little longer. So thinking, Ishanihura wrapped the precious hairs with her own and slept. Hers was not an easy sleep. Through her dreams there came and went the young girls of her mother's stories: girls who had left their little houses against the rules and custom. Some of them were bitten by snakes and died at once; some of them lived long enough to bring shame and sorrow to their families, and then died; and there was the one who cut herself and sucked her own blood and liked the taste so much, she ate more and more of herself, becoming nothing but a head—a Cannibal Head—which devoured her parents and her brothers and sisters and then rolled horribly over the earth with an insatiable need always to eat human flesh, more and more and more.

With morning and awakening, Ishanihura forgot her dreams and remembered only her desire. Night found her again in her hiding place by the pool. But that night the two brothers and her father came together, and none of the three moved or dived or swam or sat as did the shadowed one of the first night's watching. Ishanihura could barely contain her disappointment.

She was more than ever restless and unhappy and evasive during the days which followed until she went again for her time in her little house. Again she hid in her place by the pool as soon as it was dark. She waited a long time, watching the moon rise over the silent forest, and when at last there came to her ears the remembered beat of bare feet on the earth, the pool lay full in the light of the moon. Ishanihura had to crouch low to be hidden in the sparse shadow of a pine tree. Again she watched the noiseless dive, the quiet circling of the pool, the sitting by its edge and the wringing out of the hair. Shadowless and shining in the clear moonlight, the drops glistened as they were wiped down the gleaming body, and Ishanihura saw that the swimmer was Makikirèn: Makikirèn the beautiful. Now Ishanihura knew which brother it was. She knew who was the swift-moving, shadowed one, the one who swam alone.

When Ishanihura returned to the big house, she seemed almost happy, and the father and mother thought that perhaps all might yet be well. She slipped away sometimes and she was evasive about where she went and why she liked to go off alone, but, at last, she was willing to plan for the trip downriver, the trip for choosing a husband. Getting clothes and food ready and making plans suited Ishanihura, for she meant to go on a journey as soon as she could manage it—not quite the journey her parents were thinking of.

While these things were going forward inside the house,

Ishanihura was learning, outside, and bit by bit, the pattern of Makikirèn's goings and comings, the signs by which her father showed that he was expecting him, the sounds which told her he was nearby. She learned that he came home several nights of each moon to the men's house, sometimes talking and sleeping there with his father and brothers, sometimes staying only for the singing and praying, always leaving before daylight.

A new buckskin skirt and new sandals and her mother's finest mink cape were laid out ready for Ishanihura to wear. Her father explained the route she should take: she would of course go west, but then one must choose, he said. To follow the streams is sure but long, to cut over the mountains is steep and rough. Ishanihura interrupted him, "But I can't go alone. I must have someone with me!"

"Of course. You surely knew that your father expects to go with you!" It was her mother who spoke. Ishanihura's face darkened and she said, "No! My father will not know the right words to say . . ."

"Very well, my child," her father agreed gently. "I will stay here and your mother will go with you."

"My mother cannot talk to strange people. I do not wish my parents with me!"

"Then it must be one of your brothers."

"Yes! One of my brothers!"

The little ones offered to go. "Take us, elder sister!" they said. "We'll fish for you, and trap rabbits for you. Take us!"

"You are too young," Ishanihura said to them. "What would people think if I came with you?"

The older boys offered to go with her. She made an objection to each, refusing them all until at last her father said, "What is it then you want, Ishanihura?"

"I want Makikirèn to take me to the west."

"We don't know where Makikirèn is . . ."

"He is sick sometimes . . ."

"Makikirèn is far away . . ."

"He is with the Sky People . . ."

They spoke thus until Ishanihura screamed at them, "You do not speak the truth! Makikirèn is in the sweat house now! He is here. He is not sick and he is not with the Sky People! He will take me else I will not go, I will not have a husband!"

These words carried plainly to Makikirèn, who had been drawn to the house by the sound of Ishanihura's excited voice. She stopped when she saw him.

"Quiet yourself, my sister," he said to her; and to his parents, "And do you not be troubled. Let it be as she wishes. I shall go with her to the west. Who should take his sister if not her elder brother? Is all ready for the journey?"

"All is ready, elder brother."

"We shall go with the first dawn then." So it was settled and the family slept; but only Ishanihura was happy with that night's settlement.

With the first dawn, Makikirèn and Ishanihura were on their way, their carrying-baskets heavy with salmon flour, acorn bread and pounded manzanita berries, for it was a long and lonely journey, three full turnings of the sun at least, from the earth-covered house in the hills to the low-land villages.

Makikirèn was in the lead, and as the sun stood high in the sky, Ishanihura found the pace he set a wearying one. At last she put down her heavy carrying-basket and said, "Let us rest, my husband."

Makikirèn stopped. "What did you say, my sister?"

"I said let us not go so fast, elder brother."

Makikirèn kept the lead, but he went more slowly. Ishanihura, half afraid of him, half afraid of herself since her blunder, said nothing more to him, contenting herself with repeating over and over again in a sort of whispered chant to herself, "May the sun go down over the edge of the world soon! May the darkness come soon and stay long!"

At last the sun sank below the edge of the world. Their forest way was dusk and they could go no farther. The afternoon had become increasingly overcast and by sun-down there were a few drops of rain. They put their baskets on the ground and, working quickly and skillfully, Makikirèn had a little bark shelter built and a fire going by the time it began to rain in earnest, and Ishanihura had supper cooked. They ate, sheltered and warm inside, while the rain came down harder and harder outside in the surrounding dark.

Makikirèn sat by the fire after supper while Ishanihura took ferns which she had gathered earlier and spread them for their beds, hers in the shelter where they were sitting, his in a separate lean-to he had made for himself. Blowing toward her brother's eyes as she worked, she murmured a charm. "Hi – waa!" she whispered so softly he did not hear her. "May your sleep be heavy. Hi – wa – a – a!"

When Makikirèn went to his bed he was already half asleep, and as soon as his breathing became regular and heavy, Ishanihura pushed gently against his lean-to, hoping it would go over. He stirred and she whispered to him, "Elder brother, your hut is leaking. You can't sleep there. I have room. Come and sleep closer to the fire."

"No, no, I'm all right here," he answered sleepily. "I'll sleep here."

Ishanihura said no more but waited in silence till the fire gave no more light. Then she went quietly into Makikirèn's hut and lay down beside him, saying in a low voice, "Let me sleep here—my hut is leaking."

The charm she had murmured held him sleeping, his will subject to hers. He moved over to make room for her on the bed of ferns, and she lay quiet for some time. There was only darkness and the dripping of rain on bark outside and warmth within. When Makikirèn felt a woman's arms around him and felt himself being drawn over her, he dreamed. In his dream, the Sky Maiden whose lover he was came down the Sky Pole to sleep with him this night in the forest. And so it was that Makikirèn slept on, lost in his dream, and Ishanihura's desire was the only thing strong and alert and awake in the forest; and for that night, in a world filled with darkness and sleep and rain, she had fulfillment of her desire.

With dawn the rain stopped, and Makikirèn wakened clasped close in a woman's arms. It seemed to him that he was lying in a bed of ferns on the sky floor with the Sky Maiden and he turned to look at her. The woman sleeping at his side was his sister.

He stared at her, thinking back on the night just past, and as he recalled it all, despair filled his heart. Evil would come of this night, he well knew. Makikirèn restrained a first impulse to jerk away from his sister. Now at last he was awake, wholly awake, and he must think what to do; there must be no more dreaming. Thinking thus, he breathed softly on his sister's eyelids, whispering, "Hi – waa! May your sleep be long and your waking slow! Hi – wa – a – a!" Gently he unclasped her arms from around him and slipped out of the lean-to. Outside he found a piece of old pithy alder wood which had been protected by boughs and was dry. It was a medium sized log but so old that it was light and soft. He held it to himself to give it warmth from his body, then carried it inside and laid it where he had lain, and placed Ishanihura's arms so that they enfolded the alder log as they had enfolded him.

Outside once more, Makikirèn stood for a long moment, his hand on his sling, his expression thoughtful. He was remembering that his sister was one of whom it is said she carries her heart in her heel, and this is because even a tiny wound between the ankle bone and the heel is fatal to such people. He could kill her as she lay, secretly, so none would know. With her death, the evil she intended and had begun would also die and there would be an end to it. Makikirèn knew this, but he could not bring himself to do it. Instead, putting away his sling and dropping the pointed rock he had picked up a moment before, he turned his back on the woodland shelter and retraced his steps eastward to the earth-covered house, moving ever more swiftly as the distance widened between them until, once well away, his walk quickened to a trot and then to a run.

It was scarcely mid-morning when the father heard the quick running steps with their familiar cadence. He stepped outside the house to look, and a distraught Makikirèn stopped before him.

"Where is your sister?"

"Back there, back where we camped. She'll be coming home, following me. I left her where we spent the night."

"But . . . why?"

"She wanted me—and in the darkness it was as she desired. I couldn't wake up. I dreamed . . . I dreamed it was someone else. And then it was light and I left, I ran away . . ."

"A-ah-h!" And the father looked to be an old, old man as he sat down heavily on a nearby rock.

"I am afraid!" Makikirèn went on. "I do not know what she may do."

"Yes, there is no reason in her. It will go hard with us."

"What can we do, my father?"

"I do not know. I know only that I must take you all away from here, away from her." The mother had come from the house, hearing them, and he turned to her, "You agree, my wife? You know the custom?"

"I know the custom. Who better?" And the mother covered her face with her hands.

"It is decided then. But where shall we go?"

"Let me lead you up to the sky," said Makikirèn. The children had gathered round their mother and they urged her now, "O, let us go! Let our elder brother lead us to the sky!"

"Come with me to the sky," Makikirèn repeated. "We shall be safe there and the Sky People will let us live with them."

His father said, "We will go with you to the sky as soon as we've made an end to all that is here."

Without more talk, the father and his nine sons tore down the earth-covered family house, the men's house and Ishanihura's little house, and set fire to them and all they contained.

Ishanihura slept on and on in the little woodland shelter. When the spell at last released her she lay half asleep, half awake, recalling the night just past, sure in her belief that Makikirèn must love her and cling to her as she to him. Indeed he must, so her sleepy thoughts went, for now in the full light of day her arms were about him and she felt the weight of his body on hers. She stretched as she came wider awake and something stiff rolled to one side. Opening her eyes she saw that she embraced a forked trunk of pithy alder. She flung it from her crying in a choked voice, "O-O-O!" She rolled back and forth scattering the ferns which had made their bed and the bark lean-to which had sheltered them. Still crying, she got up and danced around and around the dead fire, an ugly awkward dance, tearing her hair and screaming, "O-O! I'll kill you—I'll kill you! You'll not cheat me. I'll kill you—kill you—kill!" She saw fresh footprints leading away from the fire to the east. "Ah—you've gone to warn our brothers, have you—I'll find you!" And crying and calling, running and stumbling, she started back over the trail she had followed with such strange high hopes only a sun's turning ago.

In the clearing to the east Makikirèn was saying, "Come! There is not much more time. I can hear, far off, my sister's running feet and her voice as she cries for me. Let us go quickly." Makikirèn led and the father came last, turning after each step to blow on the footprints behind; they were walking through the ashes of their home and there would be nothing to show which way they had gone. Makikirèn took them to the Sky Pole. Tall and straight, reaching from earth to sky, it stood among the trees below the pool. "Let me go first, follow close after me," he said. "You mustn't try to turn back once you are started, and if you look down you'll get dizzy and fall. Keep looking up at the sky floor and you'll be all right. Ready?"

"Yes! Yes! Let's climb to the sky!" The boys were impatient to start up.

"Come behind me, my mother. Put your hands and your feet where you see me put mine. You boys and you, my father, do the same and we shall soon be there!" Makikirèn started the climb, slowly, carefully. His mother followed him, holding where he had held, stepping where he had stepped. Behind her, one after another, came her eight sons, the father following at the end. They climbed steadily, silent except for an occasional "Coming?" from Makikirèn and an answering "Coming!" down the line from mother and children, the father answering last.

The sky floor was not far away now and Makikirèn could already see the opening in the sky, when the thud of running feet and the cries he had heard earlier as the merest breath of sound grew loud and near and came from directly underneath them. Ishanihura was home.

She stopped before the charred mass which was all that was left of the three houses. The trees around the spring were blazing and the fire spreading below the pool. Ishanihura had run home, all the long way through the forest, in a frenzy of humiliation and hate, but now, as she stared at the ruins of her home, panic began to come into her. Where were they, her mother, her father, her brothers, Makikirèn? Where could they have gone? Not a footprint could she find though she searched all around the smouldering circle of ashes. Were they in the fire? She took a stick and stirred it, and as sparks flew up she followed with her eyes their whirling, swirling course, up, up toward the sky floor. She tipped her head far back to look, and there, straight from earth to sky, was the Sky Pole, and far, far up the pole were people climbing, climbing. She knew those people. She counted—there were eleven of them, and one was a woman, her mother! They were her family!

The fire was burning all around the Sky Pole so that Ishanihura dared not try to reach its base. She stood close to the flames and called up to her family, "O, my father—do not leave me! Little brothers—come back, come back! I want to come with you, elder brother! Wait for me! Wait for me!"

Far up the pole, Makikirèn kept saying over and over, "Do not listen—do not look down. We are almost there. We are safe!"

But Ishanihura's voice came again to her mother's ears, "O, my mother! Why do you too leave me?"

"You are right my child, my one girl, what indeed do I do, leaving you alone?" Thus the mother spoke, and she looked down and saw Ishanihura. Lost in pity for her unhappy child, she continued to gaze down upon her, and as she gazed a great weariness and vertigo overcame her; she ceased to climb after Makikirèn; her hold loosened and she slipped and fell. Fell down, down from the sky to the earth, brushing from the pole and carrying with her in her fall her eight sons and her husband. Makikirèn had already stepped out onto the firm sky floor. He turned to reach a hand to his mother. There was no one on the pole. Far below in the flames he saw his brothers and his father

[ 50 ]

and mother, and, circling the flames, dancing and screaming, was his sister.

Makikirèn turned away and walked on into the sky
world, a terrible grief and bitterness in his heart. "The old
ones are right. I should have killed her in the beginning
of this thing!"

Ishanihura circled the fire, around and around, dancing
her strange stiff dance and calling out her own name, its
repeated rhythm setting the beat of her dance, "Ishanihura! Ishanihura! I-shan-i-hu-ra!"

The fire burned down to embers and she found the
charred bodies of her family—all but Makikirèn's. She
poked and raked until she was sure that his was not there.
She took their hearts, their withered and whitened hearts,
and strung them like beads of a necklace and hung them
around her neck, leaving all else to be consumed in the
hot embers.

The fire finally burned itself out and Ishanihura looked
around. Where there had been trees and houses and a
pool there was desolation, emptiness. "What shall I do?
Where shall I go?" she asked herself, and after a while
the answer came to her. "I must go to the north. Makikirèn
will be in the north. I shall look and look until I find him.
Then I shall have his heart, too!" And Ishanihura, the
string of hearts hanging about her throat, wandered off
toward the north.

Many winters came and went. Makikirèn married his
Sky Maiden and came back with her to the earth, where

[ 51 ]

they made themselves a home beside a lake far to the east of his old home. They had two sons who looked as he had looked as a child, and they were a happy family.

From time to time Makikirèn went north to hunt or to trade for treasure. Sometimes in the woods there he heard a strange, crazy, screeching cry. People said it was the Loon Woman who lived near one or another of the lakes. A fisherman told him of having seen her once. He said she was thin and mad-looking and that she wore a string of hearts around her neck as a necklace. People were afraid of her, and those who saw her ran away from her before she could come close or talk to them. Makikirèn wondered much about her—there was something familiar in her cry.

Then late one spring day, Makikirèn's two boys came running home, sure that the Loon Woman was at their own lake. He questioned them. They were frightened and he let the older boy tell him one thing and then the younger, until they were quieted. They were playing, half-hidden, in the reeds at the lake's edge. The Loon Woman came out of the forest and went to a bare sandy stretch of beach. She wore some sort of a necklace that bobbed up and down when she moved. She sat down where she could see herself in the water and leaned over, watching, as she turned her head and flapped her arms, stiff like bird's wings. And she kept singing something over and over in a screechy sort of voice. They could not understand it but it was like "I-shan-i . . ."

"What else did she say?" Makikirèn asked the boys.

"She saw us looking at her and she stopped singing—

and stared and stared—and she said 'A-ah-h,' like that. That is what she said." Makikirèn signalled his younger son to be quiet while the older one went on. "She said, 'You are Makikirèn's sons!' I said, 'Yes, we are. How do you know that?' 'Because I am your aunt and I have been looking for your father for a long, long time.' She screamed at us, 'Take me to your father! Where is your father?' Then we ran—we were too fast for her. She tried to catch us, but we got away from her. We were afraid of her. Tell me, my father, why did she say she was our aunt? Is she really our aunt?"

"I do not know," Makikirèn answered his son. "But you did right to run from her. Stay at home with your mother until I find the Loon Woman."

Makikirèn went to the lake before the first dawn. He stood half concealed in the tall reeds where he could see the lake shore. With the rising sun, the Loon Woman came to the lake from her forest sleeping-place as he hoped she might. She looked and listened, but she heard nothing, and nothing moved; she seemed to be alone. Makikirèn watched as she preened herself before her up-side-down lake image and did a stiff and awkward dance fingering her necklace. He could see her plainly, and he saw that she was Ishanihura, his sister, and that the neck-lace she wore was truly a string of human hearts. He thought of his father and his mother and his brothers, and he thought of his two young sons. He made no sound, but the air over the lake became alerted and Ishanihura looked up in alarm. Too late; the arrow had already left

[ 53 ]

the bow. Ishanihura saw her brother, the released bow in his raised hand, but in that instant, his arrow buried itself in the flesh of her foot between the heel and ankle bone, and she pitched forward into the lake. When she came to the surface, she was dead. Makikirèn recovered her body and had just brought it to shore when his sons joined him. "Were you not to wait at home until I came?" he asked them.

"Our mother said we should come now. She thought we could help you."

"So you can, since she wishes it."

"This is the one we saw!"

"You described her well."

"She is the Loon Woman?"

"Yes."

"She was our aunt?"

"She was my sister."

"Why did you kill her?"

"Because of an evil she did and would have done again. I will tell you it when you are old enough to sleep in the men's house."

"What are the ugly beads she is wearing? They look like dried hearts!"

"They are dried hearts." Makikirèn counted them. There were ten. He lifted the necklace from around Ishanihura's neck and wrapped it carefully in clean bark.

"Should we not bury our aunt?"

"Yes, at once, here in the forest." The boys helping, he carried Ishanihura's body far into the forest, burying it

[ 54 ]

away from where the children played or their mother picked berries or gathered seeds. When this was done, Makikirèn took the necklace home where he gave the hearts separate burials in the graveyard beside his own earth-covered house, the graveyard where he and his wife would sometime lie. He performed the ritual of purification for the boys and himself, and afterwards he stayed long in the sweat house alone, praying and thinking sadly of his sister. And during this time of prayer and thought, Makikirèn willed that the loon bird should forever remind his sons and his sons' sons after them of the Loon Woman.

That is why you may see a hunter kill the loon when she dances her crazy dance and calls her crazy call. And you will know he is remembering Ishanihura and is protecting his people from her ancient evil, as Makikirèn willed he should.

*Butterfly Man*

IT WAS springtime along the river and Tolowim-Woman was restless and lonely. Tolowim-Man was down-river spearing salmon. She knew that when he came home, he would join the other men in the sweat house. This was the time of the spring deer drive, the time when a woman is unclean and is avoided by her husband if he is taking part in the drive. Tolowim-Man must keep himself absolutely pure now for he was one of those who would impersonate the deer, and this is a dangerous thing to do at best. This was the time for a good wife to stay indoors and to help to see that no tabu was broken.

Tolowim-Woman was a good wife, but she remembered that spring is also the time when wild iris blooms in the hills. And Tolowim-Woman was weary of women's gossip and women's voices. So, she settled her basket hat straight on her head and let herself quietly out of her house by way of the low front passage. She took care not to jiggle or disturb the baby on his cradleboard at her back.

Once outside she stood erect, gazed briefly up and down the river, then turned away from it and walked up into the hills.

The sun was bright and hot. After walking for some time Tolowim-Woman, out of breath, slipped the carrying strap from her forehead and put the cradleboard in the shade of a manzanita bush and sat down to rest.

As she sat, a butterfly fluttered softly by. It brushed the baby's arm, causing him to laugh and try to touch it.

It brushed Tolowim-Woman's cheek and she too laughed and tried to touch it. It settled for a moment on a branch of the manzanita bush, and Tolowim-Woman, laughing again, stretched quickly forward to cover it with her seed basket. But it fluttered on to the next bush, just out of her reach. She got up from the ground, following and trying to capture it.

She wanted this butterfly as she had not wanted anything for a long, long time. It was large and strong-flying as butterflies rarely are, and it was very beautiful, with wing bands black as the mussel's shell and stripes scarlet as the woodpecker's crest.

The butterfly was so little ahead of her that each new step or reach seemed to be the one that would capture it. But always it kept its free fluttering way, just ahead, just out of reach. Nor was it flying at random, for its start-and-stop course was leading her ever up and back, farther into the hills, farther from the river.

Tolowim-Woman looked back at the baby, sleepy and comfortable in the shade of the manzanita bush. She had come a long way from him. The butterfly would tire soon now. She would make a last try for it over this next hill and take it back to the baby.

But the butterfly did not tire nor did it allow itself to be captured. Tolowim-Woman became so intent on possessing it that through the long afternoon it led her on and on. Her buckskin skirt was dirty and torn from the thorny bushes. Her cap was brushed from her head, and she did not stop to pick it up. And the heavy strings of polished dentalium and abalone shell about her neck were broken, scattered and lost.

At last as the sun was setting, and far inland, among hills she did not know, Tolowim-Woman sank exhausted to the ground. The butterfly turned at once, and fluttered back to her. It came and settled down beside her. In the dusk she saw that it was become a swift and graceful man, naked save for the butterfly girdle encircling his waist, his long hair held in a black and red headband.

Together they passed the night, Tolowim-Woman and Butterfly Man. In the morning, Butterfly Man asked her, "You wish to go with me?"

She answered, "Yes! I do."

Then he said to her, "That is good. One more day's travelling will bring us to my land, and there we shall live. But it is a long and dangerous way, O my Wife. We must cross the Valley of Butterflies and they will try to take you from me. Will you do as I say that I may lead you safely through?"

She promised to do as he told her. He said, "Follow close behind me. Step where I step. Hold tight with both your hands to my girdle. Do not let go even for a moment. And do not look at any butterfly until we are out of the valley. Obey me for this time and you shall be forever safe. Remember, I lose my power to protect you if you haven't your hands on my girdle."

They started off, Butterfly Man in the lead, Tolowim-Woman following. She grasped the girdle firmly in both her hands and she looked only at the ground. In this manner they came to the Valley of Butterflies and travelled some distance into it.

It was rough underfoot and Butterfly Man set a straight, fast course—down, across, up.

Butterflies hovered on the rocks over which they had to step. Butterflies caught against their legs and in their hair and fluttered before their faces. The air of the valley seemed to be entirely filled with butterflies.

For a long time Tolowim-Woman remembered to keep her hands in the girdle and her eyes on the pathless way underfoot. But then a butterfly, all black, larger even than Butterfly Man had been, and shining as the crow, hovered before her. He hovered just above her breasts in the line of her downcast eyes and settled for a long moment on her lips. Then he flew slowly away. She gasped with the excitement of his beauty. Her eyes followed his flight and she took one hand off the girdle and reached greedily for him.

He was gone.

But at once a hundred, a thousand others danced before her, against her eyes and cheeks and mouth. They were black and pure white and pale gold and swamp green and iris purple.

She wanted them all, and she let go her hold on Butterfly Man's girdle and reached for them with both her hands.

Not one could she catch.

Butterfly Man did not stop or look back. She kept him in sight for a time, but as she clutched ever more wildly at one and then another, she fell far, far behind him.

She ran after this butterfly and that one, here and there, up and down, stumbling, desperate, at random, always reaching for another one and always missing it.

Her hair was unbraided and tangled, her skirt kept catching in the bushes and holding her back. She untied it and threw it away. Her moccasins were in shreds. Naked except for her bark apron, dishevelled, obsessed, she continued her hopeless chase.

Butterfly Man was gone now. He was across the valley and in his own land.

Tolowim-Woman followed one butterfly and then another, on and on and on. And then her heart went away, and this was the end of Tolowim-Woman.

*Dance Mad*

It sometimes happens when many people are gathered together for dancing and singing and feasting that one or another of those who are dancing does not stop when the others stop, does not eat or sleep or rest, but goes on dancing and dancing. He goes dance mad.

Once long ago a whole people went dance mad, dancing while the moons and seasons came and went, dancing all around the world.

It began one day of spring after the heavy winds had quieted and the bare ground was green with young clover, in a village on Swift Creek, midway between the top edge of the world where the three principal rivers are small streams and the lower edge of the world where these rivers, wide and deep, flow together to make the Nom-ti-pom—that is, the Sacramento River—and empty into the sea. This village, like the sea and the rivers, was old, its people unchanged in their ways since the world was made.

The occasion was a feast celebrating the initiation into full womanhood of Nomtaimet, the daughter of one of the village families. Nomtaimet's father and mother had neglected nothing of the customary observances and training belonging to this period in a girl's life. They knew that it is an important and indeed a dangerous time for her, and for others, too, if she does not learn to keep its prohibitions, to follow its complex ritual, and to behave with decorum.

Nomtaimet's mother built for her daughter a little house. Here, separated from the family but close by, she lived alone during the moons of her initiation. She fasted and kept to herself, seeing only her mother and her mother's mother, who brought her food, bathed her, combed her hair, and cared for her, for she was not allowed, by old custom, to touch herself. She left the little house only after dark, and then briefly, keeping her head covered and her face screened from sight all the time she was outside. She spent the long days and nights inside and alone, doing only those tasks appropriate to her state, learning from her mother and her grandmother the role and behavior of a good woman and wife.

She learned that on the day and the night before her husband should go to hunt or fight or gamble, she must help him to avoid her and by no means tempt him to sleep with her, for this would spoil his luck. She learned that

[ 68 ]

she must again help him to avoid her during all of her
moon periods until she was an old woman unable to bear
him children, that she must live in her own separate house
during these times, apart from her husband. There were
further rules of continence and food prohibitions which
she must faithfully follow each time she should be with
child. Each rule and prohibition came embedded in ritual,
song, and story, and these, too, she learned.

When the long moons of learning and fasting and
praying came to an end, her mother and her grandmother
were more than satisfied with her behavior and her knowledge. They and her father, and her mother's and her
father's brothers and sisters, made a feast in her honor,
sending runners to invite the people from villages all up
and down Swift Creek to come to feast and dance and
sing with them.

Her young friends, boys and girls, had sung to her often
in the evening outside her little house to let her know she
was not forgotten, but she never broke the rule—she
neither looked out nor showed herself nor answered them.
They were as happy to have her back as she was to be
there, and now the young married women came up and
talked to her as if she was already a grown woman and
one of their group.

Nomtaimet emerged from her long seclusion pale, much
changed, and very beautiful. The old as well as the young
exclaimed at her beauty, while the old recalled that a girl
is never so beautiful as at this time when she is newly returned to the world from her long initiation. She was care-

[ 69 ]

fully dressed for her great day. Her new buckskin skirt was elaborately ornamented with shells and beads. In her ears were enormous polished shell earrings and about her neck many strings of beads which half covered her breasts. Her hair, washed and shining, hung in two thick braids tied with mink. She carried rattles made from deer's hooves and a slender willow staff given her by the young married women to symbolize her coming of age.

The women who were not taken up with cooking or caring for children gathered around Nomtaimet, admiring her. First one man and then another joined them until someone said, "We should dance—we are enough to make a circle dance." Holding hands and singing, they formed a moving circle around Nomtaimet, dancing the old circle dance which had been the coming of age dance for girls since the beginning of time.

Hearing the singing and the familiar rhythm of the shuffling side step of the dance, the old men and women came from their fires and their houses, and the children who were big enough to dance came with them, all of them joining the moving circle which grew bigger and bigger. The only ones not dancing were the women who were pounding acorns or stirring the food which was being cooked in large baskets in preparation for the feast. One by one even they put down their pestles and their stirring paddles and became part of the circle. They circled and sang until above the stamp of their dancing feet came the echo of distant voices and the silken sound of arrows flying swiftly overhead. The dancing stopped while the people from the neighboring villages appeared from behind the hills, running, shouting, and singing, the young men among them releasing arrows to whir, level, over the heads of the dancers.

In this way the guests came to the village, and there were greetings and talking and laughing until Nomtaimet's father invited them all to eat.

It was a great feast. For ten days and ten nights they ate and sang and danced. At last the feasting was over. The tenth night of singing and dancing came and went. But the pale dawn of the eleventh day found all those people still dancing. They kept right on dancing, all of them. They went dance mad.

In a long line, singing as they went, they danced up the trail leading out of the village to the east. Soon the last house was left behind and they were dancing among the hills they knew, the hills of home, up and over them until they could no longer see their houses. Through briars and chaparral, over rocks and rough ground, up and down hill, they danced on and on.

It is possible to retrace much of their dancing journey around the world, for it is known that they came to the Trinity River, the first of the great rivers, and that they forded this river as they forded all streams—by dancing straight across them. On the far side of the Trinity there is a flat, open and bare today as it was then, where the dancers again formed in a circle and danced the round dance. In a line once more, they danced on east through a gap in the hills to the Hayfork and across it and up the steep ridge beyond. At the top of the ridge they found a spring, Paukaukunmen. Here they stopped to rest and drink from the spring. You can still see the large basins in the rocks where they sat. This was their first resting place.

From Paukaukunmen, they danced down the other side of the ridge. They might have become faint from hunger, except that they learned to gather berries and to catch small animals without breaking the rhythm of their dance, crossing ridge after ridge, fording small streams, and so finding themselves at last on the banks of Middle River, the McCloud. Here they made their second resting place.

By this time their moccasins were cut to pieces and nothing much but belts and a few maple bark and buckskin shreds of aprons remained of their clothes. They did not try to replace their worn-out clothing; instead they filled their pouches with clays and dyes for face and body paint, and for the rest of their dancing trip they wore no clothes at all, keeping their faces and bodies freshly painted.

The dancers were far, far from home now, farther than any of them had ever been, in country they knew only from the tales told them by the old ones. The old ones themselves knew only so much as was learned from an occasional meeting with strangers who had, rarely and at some earlier time, wandered west as far as Swift Creek— strangers who spoke in the same tongue and observed the same way of life, but who nonetheless lived far from the center of the world and close to the borderland of peoples of other ways and tongues. The dancers found the Middle River Country much as they had been told it was, that is to say, a rich country of many people and many deer, of bushes loaded with hazelnuts and berries of many sorts. There was an abundance for all, and they hunted and gathered and ate there by the river, growing fat and sleek while they made friends with the people of the Middle River. One of the things they learned from their new friends was to catch and cook salmon—something which, strange as it seems now, they had not known about.

With this fresh salmon diet they felt new strength and new power, and they set off dancing again. They were no longer interested in hunting and gathering; they wished only to dance and dance, and then to fish and cook and eat more salmon. So now they danced close beside one stream or another, wherever the salmon were best, learning the names of the many different kinds of salmon, their size and appearance and their favorite rivers. Dancing and fishing, they went farther and farther downstream as the season drew on and the salmon swam shorter distances upstream to spawn.

Having left home in the time of winds and new clover, they had by now passed the warm moons dancing and spearing salmon. As the leaves began to dry and fall from the trees, the dancers were on the banks of the third great river, the Pitt; and dancing far, far to the south, they came where the rivers join for their trip to the sea. They were in country different from any they knew even by report from the old ones, a country whose people spoke in a tongue they did not understand. The land on both sides of the lower Sacramento River stretches as far as eye can see, marshy, swampy, full of water birds. They danced through the marshes and swamps and among the water birds until there came to them the smell of salt on the air. Leaving the marshes behind, they danced down the Sacramento where it broadens at its mouth. And they stood and watched it empty into the sea.

Wearied at last of watching, they danced again, this time on the lower rim of the earth where the river meets the sea. Keeping to the rim, they turned their backs to the river, dancing away from the Nom-ti-pom toward the north. The time of the dead leaves was past. The fog moon came and went, and it was already the time of the mud moon and of frosts. They saw all about them storms and rain and floods, but there on the lower rim of the earth there were no storms, and they continued to dance along its sometimes rocky, sometimes sandy shore.

The season of storms and cold, like the other seasons, came and went, blown away by the big winds of the awakening earth. And now the dancers turned inland, away from the sea, dancing and half blown towards home. They reached Swift Creek as the new clover was making a green mat over the earth, just as it had done when Nom-taimet first came out of her seclusion at the beginning of the dance journey.

The dancers were home, and the dance madness was no longer on them. It had lasted through all the moons and seasons and had carried them all around the world. As long as she lived, Nomtaimet told her children, as her children's children tell even today, of the feast her father made for her, and of the dance madness that came after it.

*Love Charm*

It is early morning and a young girl stands by the side of the trail, waiting, with downcast eyes. A young man comes along the trail and passes her. She does not move until he is past. Then she follows his going with her eyes and she says:

> All during the night I dream of him.
> And as soon as it is daylight
> I get up and dress
> And slip out and wait for him
> To see if perhaps he will come by.
>
> And when at last I see him coming toward me
> My heart pounds
> And I am afraid to look at him.
> I do not raise my eyes.

He passes close by me
And sometimes he gives me a flower
He has picked
Or a sweet grass he has twisted
Into a bracelet.
And I wear the flower
Even when it is wilted.
And I wear the bracelet
Until it falls to pieces.

But when he is gone again
I raise my eyes
And look at him.
And I say this charm while I look at him
So that he must come back to me.

I say:

*Suwa!*
*May you turn back*
*And look at me!*

*May you see only me*
*Wherever you look!*

*May you think about me*
*All through the day and the night!*

*May you come here to me every day!*
*May you love me as I love you!*

I say this and I cry to myself. I cry and cry.

*Umai*

THE first people were the Wogè. The world was the same in Wogè times as it is today; it has always been the same. And Umai, who was one of the Wogè, was much as our girls are now, that is to say, she was young and beautiful. But she was lonely and restless, too.

Umai's home was on the far edge of the earth by Upriver Ocean where the river begins. She liked to stand on the river bank and look out across the world. She could see down the full length of the river, from one side of the world to the other, and across Downriver Ocean to where the sun sets. She liked to wait on clear evenings for the little silver flash that follows the setting of the sun, making a brief crescent of light no thicker than the crescent of a fingernail along the horizon line. When darkness settled over the earth, Umai turned away from the river and went inside her house. She thought about the crescent of light, wondering what it was, and she thought she would like to go all the way down the river if only she could find some way to do it.

She searched here and there in her house until she found an old toy dugout canoe, no longer than her foot, no wider than her hand. She took it to the river and dipped it into the water. Then she patted its sides lightly and put a hand in and stretched the little canoe until it was two hands wide. She patted it front and back and put her foot into it and stretched it until it was long enough for both of her feet, one ahead of the other. She continued to pat the canoe and to sing to it and to stretch it a little at a time, until at last it was large enough for her to sit in.

At first dawn, Umai settled herself in her canoe and pushed off from the bank. Only then did she remember about a paddle. Having none, she held onto the sides of the canoe and swayed gently back and forth, and after a moment the canoe started down the river. In smooth water, she repeated the swaying, rocking motion. When she came to rough water or to riffles or rapids or falls, she sat still, and the canoe went safely over or around them without help from her.

She passed the Center of the World. Here, the big tributaries join the river, and the water becomes much deeper and swifter. Umai went faster and faster so that soon she was all the way downstream and at the river's mouth where it empties into Downriver Ocean.

The surf, rough and forbidding, was breaking over the rocks along the shore. But Umai looked past the breakers, out across the blue ocean and she saw where the rim of the sky meets the water. And she thought she would like to ride on the ocean, too. So she sat and counted eleven waves. As the twelfth—always the smallest wave—rolled in to shore, Umai patted the sides of her canoe and sang a song to it and swayed forward and back. The canoe rode the twelfth wave out, carrying her safely onto the open ocean. During the rest of the day she went on and on across it and farther and farther away from the earth.

The sun was low in the sky when Umai came at last to the very edge of the world. She sat in her canoe alongside the world's edge, watching quietly. She saw that the sky does not rest solidly on the ocean, but that it lifts and dips and lifts and dips in an even rhythm, except that the twelfth is a slower, gentler rise and fall. And she saw that it is this dipping sky that causes the waves in Downriver Ocean which forever beat against the shores of the earth.

The sun went down behind the edge of the world and was followed by the familiar silver flash. But from so much closer up, Umai saw that it was not at all a narrow crescent but a waving, moving something with a center of living brightness.

Umai thought: her boat had taken her easily past the pounding surf and across the great ocean—might it not carry her out beyond the world as far as this brightness?

She patted her canoe and sang to it again while she counted eleven liftings and dippings of the sky. At the

[ 83 ]

beginning of the twelfth and slower rise, Umai held tightly to the sides of the boat with both hands and rocked forward. The canoe went, straight and swift, through the gap. When the rim of the sky dipped again to the water, she was already some distance away in the Ocean-Outside-the-World.

Far away in the ocean which encircles the world, water gives way to pitch, and beyond the ocean of pitch, there is nothing at all. But where Umai went under the sky, she had only to cross a narrow stretch of water to find herself coming near the shore of the Land-Beyond-the-World.

On the shore of this land, a young girl stood waving to her—Laksis, Shining One, she was. And Umai saw that the silver brightness that follows the setting sun is Laksis waving from this far shore. She waved till Umai's canoe scraped bottom; then she helped her beach her canoe and welcomed her to her home and to the Land-Beyond-the-World.

Laksis was young like Umai and she too was lonely. Neither of them had had a friend before they found each other. They walked together over the barren and empty land and talked together as young girls talk. Umai told Laksis how from her home on Upriver Ocean she watched each night at sundown for the silver crescent behind the dipping sky. And Laksis told Umai how she came to the shore of her land each night at sundown to wave to the distant earth.

When it was time for Umai to go home, they said goodbye as friends do who will see each other again before the day is done. Together they counted eleven liftings of the sky. At the beginning of the twelfth, Laksis launched the canoe with a strong push which sent Umai back into the world under the lifted rim.

The trip home seemed very short to Umai because she was busy and happy with her thoughts. She saw that from the far side of the ocean, the earth itself looks no wider than the shore of Laksis' home. She came close to her own shore and recognized its rocks and the wide mouth of the river. It was good to see these familiar things again. Without trouble, swaying gently and singing a little, she rode a low wave through the surf and went on up the river; past its falls and rapids and riffles and into its quiet water; on to its source and her own home.

Umai belongs up where the river begins; she is known as Upriver Ocean Girl. She made no more trips in her canoe, and it shrank until it was a toy again, and Umai stored it carefully in her house. But each evening at sundown, she goes to the riverbank and she and Laksis face each other across the width of the world, and Laksis, Shining One, signals to her friend from behind the moving sky. You may see her for yourself after the sun has set —a silver streak where the sky meets the ocean, seeming no wider than the crescent of one of your fingernails.

When you are going out on the river or the ocean, it is well to sing to Umai, up there by Upriver Ocean. Put your hands on the sides of your canoe and pat it as you sing:

[ 85 ]

*Umai!*
*You rode the rapids.*
*You crossed the Ocean.*
*Lend me your canoe—*
*This is your canoe!*
*Now I too*
*Shall have no trouble*
*From the River.*
*No trouble*
*From the Ocean.*
*Thank you, Umai!*

You will then go safely anywhere: on the river or
through the surf or out on the ocean; to the edge of the
world if you want to. It will take you longer than it took
Umai: many days instead of one. And you will need a
paddle, for these are not the ancient Wogè times and you
are not a Wogè.

But you will go safely and you will come
    home safely:
If you have followed the customs and the
    rules;
And if your heart is pure.

*About-the-House Girl*

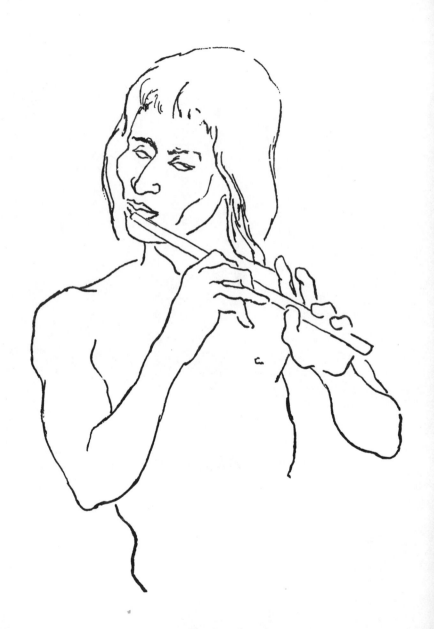

PATAPIR lived with his father and mother in a comfortable house near the mouth of the river. He liked to sit on a flat rock by the river and play his flute. The music he made carried across to the village of Rekwoi on the other side, and it drifted upstream, sometimes shrill and sharp with the trills and runs of songbirds, sometimes bright with the ripples of running water, sometimes low and sad with the soughing of the wind through the trees. He was a man grown, strong and tall, his hair reaching to his hips; but Patapir had never know any woman. He hunted and fished, he cut down trees and adzed and split the wood for sweat house or other building, he carved and burned out his own canoe and made the long storage boxes to hold his accumulating treasure, he cut and carried ceremonial wood for sweat house fires, and he sweated himself and prayed. Between working and hunting and praying, he played his flute, and songs of love and lonesomeness and longing came from his flute.

Ifapi lived far upriver with her father in the village of Merip. Her mother died when she was a little girl. Theirs was a good family and the father could have married well again had he wished to. Instead he took care of Ifapi, and the two of them lived on in their home together until she was grown—quiet, loving, and gentle. Ifapi was a shy girl who hid herself when young men came to the house. Instead of fixing on one of them as a husband for her, the father sent Ifapi to stay for some moons with an old aunt, his elder sister, who lived alone in Rekwoi. As far as the aunt's neighbors knew, Ifapi stayed indoors all day. She was never seen about the village, and when people asked for her the old woman said only that she was not well.

One day while Patapir played his flute, he kept looking across to the village of Rekwoi and up to its topmost house, far up the hill where the sun shone on it all day and where its terrace overlooked the mouth of the river, the sand bar, and the ocean beyond. This was the house of Ifapi's aunt. His mother spoke often of the aunt and sometimes of the niece who was staying with her now. Patapir had questioned his mother about the young girl but she had said that she knew nothing of her, that the old woman appeared to keep her away from men altogether, even from Patapir, although his was an aristocratic family and one long acquainted with Ifapi's people. His

mother also told him that the gossip in the village was
that the girl was not strong.

Patapir continued to think about her, wondering what
she was like, wishing he might have a glimpse of her. But
today there was no sign of a girl or even of an old woman,
and Patapir saw instead, on the terrace of a house farther
downhill, two strange young women. He put his flute on
the rock beside him and looked more closely. They were
certainly pretty, he decided, and they looked friendly sitting there sunning themselves on the terrace, their feet
tucked under, their bark skirts spread wide. He did what
he had never done before—untied his boat and crossed
the river deliberately to get acquainted with them.

The two young women had seen Patapir, even as he
had seen them. They watched while he got into his boat
and rowed across to Rekwoi. When he came up to their
terrace they were sitting as he had seen them, their feet
tucked under and their skirts spread out, and he thought
they were prettier close up than from a distance. He
spoke shyly to them, and they motioned him to sit down
on a redwood stool between them, pleased to have at-
tracted the handsome flute player. He was silent except
for answering their questions briefly, for he did not know
how to talk to them. This made them giggle, and they
chattered and flirted with him and teased him. The three
of them stayed for some time in this way, when a smell of
seaweed filled the air; not of the broken plants washed
ashore and rotting on the beach but of the deep-ocean
seaweed, whole and fresh. Patapir looked around to find

where it came from. Uphill, he saw the house of Ifapi's aunt, and the old woman herself out on her roof spreading fresh seaweed over the boards to dry. Patapir could almost taste the acrid ocean flavor, and he wanted more than anything else to have some of it to eat. He got up absent-mindedly from the stool on which he had been sitting, murmured something about seaweed and about being back soon, and left them, walking quickly to the house at the top of the hill.

As for his new friends, they shrugged their shoulders when he left them and laughed at him. "He is a strange one, the Flute Player," said one of them. "Yes, but he'll be back, you'll see," said the other.

Patapir meanwhile was greeting the old aunt whom he had known since childhood, and telling her how the smell of seaweed had drawn him up the hill to her house. She broke off a leaf, newly dried, and gave it to him, inviting him to come indoors with her. There she dipped up a small basket of acorn mush from the large one by the fire and gave it to him to eat with the seaweed. And there, for the first time, he saw Ifapi.

Ifapi lay close to the fire, a deerskin blanket covering her. She did not get up while Patapir was there. Pale and quiet, looking smaller under the heavy blanket than in fact she was, she took little part in the conversation. Nonetheless Patapir thought of her all the while he was inside the house.

He did not stay long. When he had finished the mush, he returned the basket and spoon to the old woman, thanking her and saying goodbye to her and to Ifapi. Then he went back down the hill to the two young women. As soon as they saw him one of them asked him, "Where did you go?" And the other one asked him, "What is so interesting up the hill there?"

"I was talking with the old woman in the upper house," said Patapir. "She gave me some mush and seaweed." The girls shrugged their shoulders and looked at each other and laughed. Patapir stopped for only a few minutes with them before crossing back to his side of the river. During the rest of the day he cut and carried loads of wood for a sweat house fire, and at the end of the day he played long, long on his flute.

While he played he made plans for the next day, and in the morning he crossed the river as soon as he saw his new friends out on their terrace. He said to them, "I want to sleep with you. May I come to your house tonight?"

The young women laughed when he asked this, and one of them said, "Don't try to fool us—you are only pretending you want us." And the other one said, "You really want that girl up the hill. You just come here to be near her!" But after more teasing, they agreed that he might come. "Come tonight." . . . "But wait till it is dark!" they told him.

Patapir fished during most of the day. Then he sweated himself again. As the sun neared the rim of the sky he was restless, already seated in his canoe waiting to paddle across as soon as the sun was set. Thus it happened he was outside the young women's house before they were expecting him. They were dressing, calling back and forth to each other while they dressed. Patapir stayed at a little distance from the house, but even so their voices reached him plainly: "How shall we dress tonight?"

"We could wear our good skirts."

"Or our new aprons."

"No one can see what we wear in the dark. Why not the same as last night?"

"But we must be sure to take capes. It is cold on the water." This was the way they talked.

Patapir waited, and the young women came out onto the terrace dressed for the out-of-doors and carrying canoe paddles. They stopped when they saw that Patapir was there, but before he could say anything they began to laugh, and then they ran as fast as they could away from him, downhill. He ran after them but it was already dark. He heard men's voices calling softly to them from the river, and as he came out onto the bank the girls were already seated with several men in a canoe which was headed downstream, one of a long line of canoes filled with men and an occasional woman or two, and being paddled toward the mouth of the river. Last of all there came a small canoe with only two men in it. They called to Patapir as he stood, uncertain what it all meant, and what he should do. "Come. Come with us," they said. "We have plenty of room."

"But where do you go?"

"To the dancing across the ocean! Come!"

Patapir got into the canoe. He saw that there were blankets for keeping warm, pipes for smoking when they should wish to rest from paddling, and baskets for gathering fresh seaweed.

The canoes, ten in all, cleared the bar and the offshore breakers and set out to sea. They stopped once at a large sea stack to rest and fill their baskets with seaweed and to have a smoke. Patapir noticed that where they knocked out their pipes the grass and flowers growing in the crannies of the rock were charred, showing that pipes had been knocked out there many times before.

Beyond the sea stack, they paddled steadily on, ten boats one after another to the edge of the world where sky and ocean meet. Patapir watched, breathless, as the boats lined up side by side. Truly it was as his grandfather had told him: the sky moves up and down, up and down; when it drops it strikes the ocean with a force so strong it starts the waves which beat unendingly against the shores of the distant earth. Patapir counted, and as his grandfather had told him, every twelfth lifting of the sky was slower than the in-between ones, leaving a gap for a long enough time that a canoe, set and ready, could pass under the sky, out beyond the edge of the world and into the outer ocean. This the ten boats lined up at the edge succeeded in doing, counting the waves, and going under as one with the slower wave. Patapir looked back. He saw that the sky was again down against the water, and that he and his companions were outside the world, paddling through the waters of the outer ocean. They went as far

as the Land-Beyond-the-World, where they beached
their canoes on the flat and sandy shore.

There was a fire up the beach a short distance and a
circle of people around it watching a Life Renewing
Dance. Patapir and the others from the ten boats went to
the fire and stood quietly where they could see the dancing.

As he watched, Patapir wondered why this that was so
new and strange seemed somehow familiar. Then he recalled that it was the dancing the old ones in the sweat
house at home told him of when they were in a mood to
talk to him of their own youth. He had thought their tales
of dancing across the ocean to be no more than old men's
imaginings about bygone days. They told him that such
night voyages down the river and over the sea were only
for the young and the strong, and they hinted that sometimes a man persuaded his sweetheart to go along. They
spoke of this adventuring as something in the past—their
past, when they were young and carefree, hunting and
fishing by day, and paddling across the ocean and outside
the world, dancing and making love by night—a time
when sleep was something for the old.

Patapir was wide awake and aware and alive as never
before—what had been the old one's dream was become
his own reality. Never had he imagined such dancing and
such singing. The singing rose from a low wail to the
strident shrillness of the highest notes of songbirds. The
rhythm of the dancing feet was strong and pure and
steady on the earth. There was beauty and authority in

the voice and gestures of the Leader as he offered incense
and tobacco to fire and to Spirits, and recited the prayers
for each.

Patapir and his two companions in the canoe were seeing this for the first time. So interested were they, they
pressed forward, nearer to the fire, nearer to the dancers.
By now, the men from the other canoes had joined the
line of dancers. Patapir saw that the old ones spoke truly
—the dancers were all in their young manhood, strong
and tall. Some of them could leap in the dancing, high,
and with the long-legged grace of the crane; and some
could sing, sending their voices higher than the flickers'
call. Little by little, Patapir forgot the dancers and singers as his attention gathered more and more about the
person of the Leader's assistant. This was scarcely surprising; the young men beside him had eyes for nothing
else, nor did Patapir, once he really looked at her.

Women never dance in the Life Renewing Dance, but
the Leader is served by one woman who makes and tends
the fire for him, hands him angelica root and tobacco and
his pipe, removing them when he has taken what he
wants of the incense or finished the pipe ritual. It is a position of honor for a woman, and since she must not have
borne a child and must submit to training, to prescribed
diet, and to purification, it follows that the Leader will
select her with care. She is sure to be young and good-
looking, with proud bearing, gracious and graceful.

The assistant Patapir was gazing at was young, the delicate oval of her face shadowed by shyly lowered lids, the

[ 97 ]

young breasts shadowed by long hair braided and tied with mink and by the cloak she wore over her shoulders— a cloak made of hundreds of closely sewn crests of the red-headed woodpecker, seeming itself a sheet of flame from the fire as she moved. Her skirt and front apron were heavy fringes of shells strung close together, each string tufted with a red woodpecker crest. She was barefoot, and as she bent to the fire or lifted a basket of incense to the Leader, the play and motion of thigh and leg showed through the fringe of shells which answered her every movement with a low rustle as of a receding surf playing shell against shell on the beach.

She brought a piece of driftwood and put it on the fire, facing Patapir as she did so. The fire blazed high, lighting her shadowed face, and Patapir saw that she was Ifapi— Ifapi, the little pale girl whom he had seen lying in the old woman's house at home. She did not raise her eyes or look at him, but for the rest of that night's dancing he watched her, and during the early morning hours of paddling home, back under the sky rim and all the way across the ocean, he thought of her.

He went far into the hills that same day, cutting the topmost branches of tall fir trees according to old ceremonial rule, bringing them home in bundles. With these he made a sweat house fire, and sweated and prayed until almost sundown. Then he swam and washed himself in the river, and when the sun was quite gone, he crossed to the other side in his canoe. The aroma of drying seaweed wafted down to him, pungent and sea-filled, and he went uphill toward the old aunt's house.

Patapir had quite forgotten the two young women who had seemed so pretty to him the day before, but they were waiting for him on their terrace. He spoke to them and they knew from his manner that he was not meaning to come in with them this time. One of them said, "I don't believe you have come to see us at all. You don't even want to stop and talk!" And the other one said, "You only want to see the girl who is sick all the time up there with the old woman!"

Patapir, whose thoughts were far away, answered them, "Yes. She is the one I want to see," and he went on without more talk. They laughed, shrugging their shoulders and turning their backs to him.

When Patapir got to her house the old woman was on the roof gathering in the dried seaweed. She gave him a leaf and invited him inside to have some of her acorn mush. He followed her through the round door and there, just as before, he saw Ifapi covered with the heavy blanket, looking pale and ill. Her aunt climbed down the ladder into the pit to see if the mush was done, and Patapir jumped lightly after her, going to Ifapi, and patting her shoulder to draw her attention. Ifapi turned toward him; but before she could speak, her aunt saw what he was doing and spoke up sharply. "Do not touch her," she said. "She is very sick. You mustn't ever do that again!" She could not think what was in Patapir's mind, and she was

[ 99 ]

frightened, unable for the moment to move, a wooden stirrer still in her hand, watching him and repeating over and over, "You mustn't . . . she's sick . . . she's always sick . . . you can't . . ."

Patapir paid no attention to her. He slid his arms carefully under the blanket on which Ifapi lay, lifted her, deerskin blanket and all, and carried her up the ladder. Only then did he speak to the aunt, saying, " I know that she is not sick! I saw her at the dancing across the ocean last night."

This brought the old woman back to herself. She threw aside the stirrer and followed Patapir up the ladder. Taking his arm, she said imploringly to him, "Then go—go outside. . . . Leave her!" Patapir shook his head, but she held him still. "Leave her I say! I must speak with her— only for a breath—I will call you back. . . . Please to do what I say—this is the right thing, I tell you!"

Patapir had had every intention of carrying Ifapi off without talk or delay, but something in the old woman's tone made him listen to her; and when he turned to Ifapi, she nodded her head and, in a voice so low he scarcely caught her words, said to him, "Do what she says."

"Call me then," he said, leaving Ifapi and stepping outside. And before his impatience drove him back, the aunt called him in.

Stooping to go through the low door, he looked first for Ifapi. She was there, but the shadowed face was no longer pale and indifferent, but awake as at the dancing. She was dressed in the shell fringe skirt and apron, and the red-crested feather cloak was around her shoulders. Patapir went to her and took her arm, but the old aunt's voice interrupted, "Flute Player of Rekwoi, what are you doing?"

"I am taking this little one with me, aunty."

"Wait! Let the shadows grow longer while I tell you . . ."

"Tell quickly, aunty, for I would be away from here . . ."

"Flute Player, this child is not an old woman's nobody. She has a father, my brother, upriver. I must answer to him for her, and you must answer to him for her."

"This I know, aunty. My father knows the brother of whom you speak."

"There is another thing that I must tell you so you do not misjudge me. It was she and not I who wished to make this look of sickness. I helped her to it only because she begged me to."

"I believe you, old woman, and I believe that, just now, she laid aside her sickness of her own wish. Isn't that true?"

"It is true, Flute Player. But what do you do with her?"

"Do you not worry, aunty. I am taking her with me and I am marrying her—tonight. But tomorrow, as soon as it is light, we shall go upriver, she and I, and her bride price goes with us to her father. You've known me all my life, aunty, and you know my father and my mother. You and her father and the Leader across the ocean will say she was proudly bought."

The old woman had to content herself with this promise. She was wise as well as old, and she knew that she could do very little, for what Patapir wished, Ifapi wished also. She looked on without interfering when Patapir went to Ifapi and again took her arm, saying, "Come!"

Ifapi said, "Goodbye, aunty. Thank you for helping me. I shall tell my father that you were very good to me."

Ifapi followed Patapir through the low round door. On the terrace, he lifted her gently into his arms, the feather cloak flowing about them like a flame as he carried her into the darkness, down the hill to the river, to his canoe. They crossed to his side of the river, and there in a hollow under a redwood tree he made a soft sweet bed of ferns laid over with deerskin rugs, and there he and Ifapi spent their wedding night.

In the early dawn, Rekwoi was a village asleep. No one stirred or wakened as Patapir stowed his long boxes of treasure in the canoe or as he and Ifapi took their places at either end and headed upstream. He pulled against the current, and the strong smell of seaweed again filled his senses as in a remembered dream, while far up the hill an old woman spread fresh seaweed over her roof and watched the sun rise above the canyon wall and a canoe move out of her sight upriver, disappearing behind the same canyon wall.

Paddling steadily, stopping for short rests, Patapir and Ifapi came to her old home. Ifapi ran ahead to greet her father. He was surprised to see her, and he questioned her, saying, "All is well?"

"All is well, my father."

"What brings you home?"

"That you may know my husband."

Her father sighed, speaking half to himself, half to Ifapi, "Ahhh—that old woman, my sister, she was not careless with you?"

"No, no, my father. She was good to me and cared for me and helped me."

"But then whom could you have married? I have heard nothing of any man looking at you—only that you were serving the Leader across the ocean . . ."

"So I have served him—I alone." Ifapi said this with quiet pride.

"Tell me then—who is this man, your husband—you must know, my child, that when I let you go away from me, it was with the foolish thought that you might continue to keep yourself from men, and that the Flute Player of Rekwoi might one day come to know of your being chosen by the Leader and wish to marry you. I know his family, and perhaps you have not forgotten how we used to listen together to his songs as they floated up the river—before you were grown and went away from me."

"It was as you say, my father. I hid from men, going only to the dancing, and I, too, thought always of the Flute Player. At last, he saw the dancing—and wished to marry me."

Patapir then came up to Ifapi's father to greet him and to offer the boxes of treasure, his bride payment for Ifapi. As he had promised the old aunt, he brought a proud man's payment for a beloved daughter.

The father was satisfied. He said, "It is good, my son-in-law, my daughter."

The young people stayed with Ifapi's father until it was time to dance the Life Renewing Dances again. The father was much beyond the age of those who usually make the long voyage, but his heart was set on hearing his son-in-law sing there. He had heard Patapir singing alone in the hills, practicing against the calls and whistles of the birds, and he knew that it was a good voice for the sacred songs. So they were three in Patapir's canoe. Other canoes joined them farther downstream until there were ten of them in all. As on Patapir's first trip, they cleared the bar and went the way of the setting sun, stopping for a rest and a smoke at the lonely rock, and then going on—one boat after the other—across the ocean, under the sky rim and across the outer ocean to the Land-Beyond-the-World.

There was such dancing and singing that night as those who stood in the circle never forgot. For Ifapi, it was the last time she might make and tend the fire, the last time she might offer incense and tobacco and pipe to the Leader and receive these back from his hands, the last time she might move in and out of the line of dancers, the one woman in the sacred ceremony. Before another season of the Life Renewing Dances she would no longer be eligible to serve at them. But Ifapi was without regrets or sadness. The eyes of all the men followed her this night as never before, for the oval face was unshadowed. Whenever she raised her arms to the Leader to give him a basket or to take his pipe, she raised her eyes, too, to look down the line of dancers to the new one there, the one with the voice so strangely low and high like a flute—to Patapir, her husband.

The two young women of Rekwoi were at the dancing that night, and this is how it went with them. They watched and saw how beautiful Ifapi was, and they listened and heard the new voice among the singers. They crowded nearer and nearer, and looking in the direction Ifapi looked, they saw Patapir. They stared a long time at him. At last, one of them said, "That new singer there—he looks like the young man across the river from us." And the other one said, "Yes. Of course. He is the one we tease all the time." Then the first one said, "I didn't know he could sing. All he ever does around home is to play his old flute and go see that sick girl up the hill." Her companion answered, "He'll go and see her again—the sick one—you just see if he doesn't!"

One of the men standing in the circle interrupted their talk. "Yes, that is the Flute Player of Rekwoi. Everyone knows him because of his playing."

A second man said, "But don't you Rekwoi people know? She," motioning toward Ifapi, "she is the 'little sick girl.' The Flute Player married her, and took the bride price to her father in Merip—my village. No one in our time has given treasure to equal it. The father is well satisfied."

"*She* is the sick girl . . . *He* is married . . ." The young women could only repeat this over and over. They looked at one another, but they did not shrug their shoulders this time.

When the men said, "We must start home, we have far to go before daybreak," the young women did not answer them. They felt such fools they had slipped away and were never seen in Rekwoi or at the dancing again. Only their little round basket hats were left lying on the ground, marking the place where the girls were last seen.

The long night of singing and dancing came to an end at last. Patapir and Ifapi and her father went off somewhere, and for half a moon's time no one saw them or knew anything of them. Then one morning Patapir's parents sighted their canoe far out at sea, seeming to skim the water like a bird, and soon it was over the bar and they were home once more. Patapir put into the canoe the long boxes which held his dance outfits and treasure, his ten precious sacks of sacred tobacco and his flute. When they were ready to leave again, Patapir's parents asked him where they meant to go, and he answered, "Far across the ocean in the wake of the fresh seaweed! Do not worry. You will have word of us and know that all is well."

His father and mother cried when the canoe with its three passengers and its load of treasure went out over the bar, on and on like a sea bird, out of their sight and knowledge.

Patapir spoke truly when he said they would have word of him, for he was the great singer in the sacred ceremonies in the Land-Beyond-the-World for many, many moons. News of him and his family came over the bar to Rekwoi and on upriver as far as the music of his flute used to carry—all the way to Merip—as often as the ten canoes returned from the dancing.

We know that Patapir and Ifapi lived out their lives in that far land beyond the sky rim, and that Ifapi and her children and her father, as long as he lived, came with Patapir to the dancing. And we know the pet name Patapir gave to Ifapi. Because he never forgot the first time he saw her, he named her "About-the-House Girl."

*Tesilya, Sun's Daughter*

THERE is a variety of large cane growing in brakes and thickets along the Colorado River which, beyond its many practical daily uses, is said by the river people to possess a powerful magic for one who knows how to use it. This cane is named for Ahta, a hero who lived in the far-off times. Nowadays the story of Ahta (Cane) and of Ahta-hana (son of Cane) is renewed for the river people of each generation in a dream which comes to one or another of them, usually to someone already skilled in the practice of magic and story-telling.

The dream is of Ahta and his son, their journeyings and fights and great exploits. Only by the way does Tesilya, the wife of Ahta, or indeed any woman come into the dream at all.

Of Tesilya we know only that she was beautiful and gracious, that she was joyous when her world was good, that she was quiet and strong when her world was evil, that she was so in age as in youth. And perhaps that is as much as a dream need tell of a woman.

The dream usually begins with Ahta already grown, living with his elder brother Hotpa and his uncle in the shadow of the sacred mountain of the river people.

The uncle watched over the two boys with loving care. Hotpa was skilled in magic, but his uncle saw with sorrow that he was cruel and of an unhappy disposition, and that he was already jealous of his younger brother, knowing as he did that Ahta was born a hero, that he was gentle and brave, and beloved of all who knew him.

Each night the three of them came home to an empty, cheerless house, the food for the evening meal yet to be cooked. At last the uncle said, "Look at us! We are three men here with no woman. We come home and there is no wood, no water, no food. I am old. But go, you two young ones, tomorrow, and find, one or both of you, a wife."

The brothers took their uncle's advice, and early the next morning set out, travelling east from the sacred mountain. Ahta had heard of old man Sun's daughter, and it was in his mind to find her.

They walked all day and slept the night on the open desert. As soon as it was light they went on again, always east, until toward midday they reached Sun's house. Ahta and Hotpa stopped before its door of plaited willowbark.

Tesilya, Sun's daughter, lived there with her father.

Sun was often away from home and Tesilya had as a pet and guardian a yellow-hammer woodpecker whose cage hung high above the door. No one but Tesilya ever touched the yellow-hammer, and if a stranger approached or if all seemed not right when she was alone inside, he cried out in his hoarse voice and beat against the sticks of his cage to warn her.

This morning, though two strangers came up to the door, the yellow-hammer made no sign, no sound. Ahta lifted down his cage and took him out, and it was only after he had set him on the ground in front of the door that the bird gave his usual cry. Tesilya heard the hoarse, familiar voice, and glancing warily between the willow plaits, she saw where he was. She remembered that this was a sign that someone outside there wished her for his wife—someone the yellow-hammer was not afraid of—so she looked much more closely from behind her screen.

She looked first to the north, and there she saw Ahta standing, facing her door expectantly. Then she looked to the south where Hotpa stood, also facing her door expectantly. Her bright gaze turned back to the north, to Ahta the young hero. As she looked toward him a second time, she laughed softly. This made the brothers laugh aloud and caused the yellow-hammer to sing. And so they waited as they were, the brothers and the woodpecker, for the willow screen to be lifted.

They had to wait quite a while. First Tesilya poured water into a bowl blackened inside with charcoal. Using this for a mirror, she made herself up carefully. She painted two small red triangles on her forehead between the arched black eyebrows and the short black bangs, and with the same red, a small curving-out bow down each cheek. Then she encircled her eyes and breasts with narrow lines of yellow paint. She dressed herself in a new fringed willowbark skirt and a new little front apron, fringed also, and a wide braided belt. She put earrings in her ears and hung many heavy strings of beads around her neck and wrists. Close about her throat she clasped an enormous clam shell, carved in a frog pattern. She tied two small bags of face paint, one red, one yellow, to her belt; and she peeled a fresh willow switch with which to sweep her skirt smoothly under her so as not to crumple it when sitting.

Ready at last, she raised the slatted screen and came out of the house. First, she picked up the woodpecker and put him back in his cage; then, with the cage on her arm, she went to Ahta and stood before him and looked into his face. Ahta was smiling, and she was smiling, too.

Ahta asked her if she would go home with him to the sacred mountain, and she answered, "Yes. I am ready to go."

Hotpa was angry. He grabbed Tesilya's arm, shouting, "She is mine! She is mine! I am older than you and she is mine!"

But Ahta held Tesilya and would not give her up. He said, "No. She chose. She came to me. She belongs to me."

Hotpa struck Ahta and tried to drag Tesilya away from him but Ahta was too strong for him and beat him off. At last Hotpa stopped dragging at her and fighting his brother and said, "Very well! Let us go home."

They started in the direction of the sacred mountain, but they had not gone many steps west when Tesilya stopped and looked back to her home. "I thought my house was already far away, but it is only a little distance," she said. "Will you wait, you two, while I sing the song of my house?" The brothers waited and listened to Tesilya's song. She sang of her father, his house, and her life there as a child and a young woman, and of how she was leaving now, never to return, never to see her father or the house again.

Her song finished, they turned again to the west and walked on all through the day. As they walked, the brothers sang to Tesilya to make the way seem shorter. They sang her the song of Mountain Sheep and the song of Vulture and the songs of all the other stars until the stars themselves came out and night was upon them, far from any house or people.

Ahta made a bed on the open desert and took Tesilya to it. As in the morning, Hotpa fought with his younger brother over her, but again Ahta was too strong for him. In the end, Hotpa went off and slept alone, and in the morning Tesilya was much relieved to have him speak to her as "My Sister-in-law."

The three of them continued their journey in the morning, and when the sun was overhead they reached the sacred mountain, and there outside their house, they found their uncle sitting, waiting for them.

Tesilya was shy before her new uncle and hid her face behind her hair which hung, black and shining, almost to her knees. The uncle took her hand in greeting between both of his. Then, gently, he parted the heavy hair and uncovered her face, saying, "Come! Let me see my younger brother's daughter-in-law!"

He led her into the house and showed her over her new home and talked to her in his quiet way. Shyness left her, and soon she was grinding corn, singing as she worked. The three men smiled, repeating to one another, "See how beautiful she is!"

When it was supper time, the uncle helped Tesilya make mush of the fresh-ground corn. He poured the corn slowly into the pot of boiling water while she stirred it and added salt. Together they tasted it to be sure it was right.

From that time, when the men came home they found a warm fire and fresh water and a supper ready, and a happy woman singing at her work. But when it was bedtime the uncle saw the soreness in Hotpa's heart renewed each night, for Tesilya went always with Ahta to the southwest corner of the house, which was his sleeping place. The uncle did what he could. When he learned that his friend Jaguar had a marriageable daughter, he sent the two brothers to the west to Jaguar's house to bring her as wife to Hotpa. And so, at last the uncle thought his household was complete and at peace. When he settled himself for the night on his pallet at the center of the house, Ahta would be lying in his corner with Tesilya, and Hotpa in his with Jaguar's daughter.

But there was to be no peace in this house. Hotpa could not forget his humiliations in the journeys with Ahta. It had happened at Jaguar's house as at Sun's house: Jaguar's daughter, too, had chosen Ahta first, and it was only when Ahta said that he did not want her that she turned to Hotpa. Even when this was all past and over and Jaguar's daughter was his wife and content, Hotpa could not forgive Ahta and Tesilya. He hated them as together they became ever more beautiful, and happiness was in them, and all the river people loved them. In their happiness they forgot to fear and to watch Hotpa.

Hotpa put a powerful ghost illness on Ahta, which no one recognized for a magic spell until it was far advanced. It caused Ahta to have terrible nightmares; then he became delirious, and at last mortally weak. Secretly, Hotpa kept a close watch on his younger brother. There came a morning when Tesilya and the uncle left Ahta alone for a while. He was asleep, and in any case too weak to cry out or to defend himself. With savage swiftness, Hotpa cut off a piece of Ahta's scalp, and, while his brother yet lived, hacked out the shinbone and kneecap from one of Ahta's legs. Tesilya was not gone for long, but when she returned, this violence had been done, Hotpa was nowhere to be seen, and her husband Ahta was dead.

Hotpa, a man possessed, waved the bloody shinbone over his head, and running from house to house, called out to whoever was inside to come with him for a game of

[ 117 ]

shinny. Threatening and promising, he found players for his shinny game, for he was greatly feared. Never was there such a game, for Hotpa used Ahta's shinbone for a shinny stick, and his kneecap for a ball.

But when the people found that Ahta was dead they fled in panic from Hotpa, out onto the desert. And Hotpa and his shinny players ran away from the sacred mountain, too, hiding in the mountains far to the north. Jaguar's daughter did not go with Hotpa. She went home to her father's house in the west, and the old uncle and Tesilya were left alone.

Alone, they did all that must be done for a hero's passage from this world. When they had sung the songs for the newly dead and performed the other rites, they laid Ahta's body on a funeral pyre along with his clothing and blankets and ornaments, his bows and arrows and his war clubs: everything that had belonged to him. They burned everything, even his house, in a great and inclusive and cleansing fire which translated him wholly into the world of the dead. They cut their hair to mourning shortness, and together they cried and sang the mourning songs for Ahta, and cried and sang and cried again. They built themselves another house and lived on there, mourning and missing him always in their hearts.

The moons came and went until one morning Tesilya wakened in heavy pain. Her uncle cared for her gently as a loving woman might, and he told her that her baby would be born soon. The day passed and night came and the baby was not yet born, but they heard him plainly, singing and talking inside her. This frightened Tesilya, but her uncle reassured her. "This is good," he said to her. "It means that your son will have much power and be a hero."

Toward dawn of the next day the baby stopped singing and spoke plainly, saying, "Be quiet, you two! Let no one come near! I am coming out into the world."

And so it was that the son of Ahta and Tesilya was born. His great-uncle laid him gently on a bed of warmed sand and covered him to his neck with more warmed sand, that he might rest and become accustomed to the outside world. Tesilya saw that her son was beautiful and like his father, and she named him Ahta-hana.

The night Ahta-hana was born, it rained and rained in the mountains where Hotpa was hiding, although it was not the season of rainfall. Hotpa took this to be some sort of a portent. He sent a messenger to see if Tesilya's baby had been born. If so, and if it were a boy—something Hotpa greatly dreaded—he meant to have the baby killed.

The baby's great-uncle was sitting in the doorway when the messenger arrived before Tesilya's house. He greeted him courteously and listened while the messenger told him that Hotpa wanted to know how Tesilya fared, and if her baby was born.

"Yes. She was born last night," said the uncle. "I will bring her for you to see so that you can tell Hotpa of his niece." So saying, he went into the house, returning shortly with Ahta-hana, bound to a cradleboard with the diamond pattern of cross-strapping used only for girl babies. He even gave the baby on its board to Hotpa's messenger to hold, all the while appearing at ease and open.

The messenger returned to Hotpa, telling him that his brother's child was a girl, and Hotpa's fears were put to rest.

Once he was born, Tesilya's baby did not talk as he had in her womb. Within six days he smiled and within twelve days he laughed aloud. With the return of the moon of his birth he ran about alone and talked plainly. During the passing of many placid seasons he grew under the tender care and teaching of mother and great-uncle, without particular event to mark the seasons.

But the time came when Hotpa could no longer stifle the homesickness of those who had fled with him, and he returned with them to the sacred mountain.

Ahta-hana was much interested in these people, new to him. Tesilya dressed him in a girl's willowbark skirt and let him go among them. Hotpa gave him a doll carefully carved from bone, and Ahta-hana watched his uncle's people play shinny. When Tesilya was putting him to bed that night, he showed her his new doll and he told her of the new sort of shinny game his uncle's people played.

Tesilya knew there was evil in all this. She said nothing that night or the next or the next. But the fourth night, when she was talking to Ahta-hana at his bedtime, she told him the truth: that the bone doll, the shinny stick, and the shinny ball were made from his own father's bones. It saddened and dismayed Tesilya to do this, but she had no power to protect her son, and she feared greatly for him.

Ahta-hana cried all through the night, and when it was light he wandered out onto the desert still crying. Worn out, he crept under a mesquite bush and went to sleep. As he slept, he dreamed that a beetle crawled off a branch of the mesquite bush to his upper lip. There the beetle sat and talked to him, telling him all about his father and his father's death.

When he wakened, Ahta-hana lay quiet awhile thinking over his dream. At last he understood the meaning of Hotpa's shinny game. And he understood that Hotpa would surely destroy whatever had been dear to his dead brother.

Ahta-hana laid aside his girl's willowbark skirt and went home to his mother and great-uncle, and when he spoke to them they knew he was no longer a child in his mind.

They listened to Ahta-hana's words, and they did as he said. His great-uncle was to stay as always by the sacred mountain. To his mother, Ahta-hana said, "But you, my mother, you must go back to my grandfather's house. My uncle will try to kill you; he will surely harm you if you stay here. Go—and when I have done all I must do, I will come to you."

Tesilya filled her mirror bowl with glowing coals from the fire. She would replenish the coals with twigs and sticks from time to time as she travelled. Holding it close to her, it would warm her and light her way across the

desert. She said a quiet goodbye to her uncle and to her
son. Without tears that could be seen, without a backward glance, Tesilya opened the door of her house and
stepped outside. Straight and firm, she walked to the east,
the bowl of coals held in both her hands. She walked back
over the way she had come with Ahta, toward the house
she had thought never to see again.

Ahta-hana watched her until he could no longer catch
the faintest glimmer from the bowl of glowing coals, far,
far out on the desert. Then he cried, "O, why have I sent
my mother away like a bird?

> "A bird's nest is on the desert.
> It sleeps on the desert
> Where no one lives."

And Ahta-hana cried and sang songs of lonesomeness
for his mother.

Tesilya found her way back to Sun's house, and, again
with a yellow-hammer for a pet, she lived on, dreaming
of Ahta-hana, fearful of all that might befall him, waiting
for him to return to her some day as he had promised.

As soon as Tesilya was safely out of reach of Hotpa and
his evil magic, Ahta-hana did the only thing he would be
able to do until more age and wisdom and power were
his: he hid himself close to the shinny field, and when
the play passed his way, he stole the shinny ball. No one
saw him take it or run home with it. The players were
still looking for it in the grass when Ahta-hana appeared
outside his house door, the ball in his hand. Hotpa dared

not interfere while Ahta-hana offered the kncccap ball to the Four Directions, singing a prayer to each, nor when he laid it on the ground and struck it as hard as he could with a cane such as his father had carried. The ball flew like a meteor to the west, falling somewhere in the mountains there. This done, Ahta-hana went indoors and was not seen any more. Hotpa came to kill him, but he found only his old uncle alone in the house. His uncle told him that Ahta-hana had gone to be with his mother in Sun's house, and Hotpa was afraid to follow him there.

Ahta-hana went on a long journey which took him to the very end of the earth where it meets the ocean. He learned many things on his travels. He came to know the properties of plants and springs and mountains and deserts. He subdued Rattlesnake, and thereby his own fears. He crossed and re-crossed the Colorado River until it was no longer a barrier, and its total course was known to him. He reached the sea, staying there until the shells along its shore and the life in its waters seemed no longer strange to him, but were known and within his control, just as he came to know the water birds, so different from the birds of the desert.

At last he turned his steps toward home. Wisdom and magical power and doctoring skill were now his. Young as he was, he was already full grown, for he had grown at a hero's rate of growth. Around his neck he wore many strings of shell beads and a thick feather rope, and on his head a headdress of square-clipped raven's wings. He was as beautiful as his father before him.

On his return journey, he encountered Kwayu the Cannibal and Kwayu's four daughters, all of whom fell in love with him. Because they so much wished it, and he felt sorry for them, he married them all even though the eldest of the sisters was his favorite and the one of his own choosing.

Now Ahta-hana was weary of wandering, and it seemed to him that he had surely learned enough that he might return home. He dreamed, and afterwards he said to his wives, "I know that my mother is dreaming of me. I must go to her." All four wives wished to go with him and he consented to their going. But it was as he had feared, their strength and endurance were far less than his, and he felt so much encumbered by them that he thought of leaving them and going on alone. To make this appear more reasonable, he caused a cold rain to fall, until they could scarcely drag their feet through the mud. He went on ahead; but he looked back and saw them still struggling after him. He was ashamed of what he had willed and done, and he knew at last that he truly loved them. For the remainder of the journey he made no more cold rains; rather he learned something of their needs and natures as he had of other life in the world different from himself, and he was no longer impatient with them nor did he think again of leaving them behind.

For many days they travelled north, until one morning a yellow-hammer flew out of the east toward them. He flew straight to Ahta-hana who took him in his hands, saying, "This must be my mother's pet, and the bird who guards her. That is why he comes to me. My mother cannot be far from here." They turned to the east, going the way the woodpecker had flown, and by noon of that day they reached Sun's house with the willowbark door, and the bird cage hanging there in its old place. Ahta-hana set the yellow-hammer on the ground outside the door of Sun's house, as had his father long, long ago. And the bird gave his familiar, hoarse cry.

Tesilya came to the door to look through its slats. When she saw Ahta-hana, she raised the door and ran to him, holding him close and crying, "My son—it is you! The time was so long—I thought you must have been killed—I thought I was never to see you again!" She stood back a little from him and looked at him. She saw that he was become indeed beautiful and a hero, and she said exultingly, "You have dreamed well! It is good!" Then she turned to greet her son's wives, saying apologetically to them, "You have come far and stood long. You are tired. Sit down. When you have rested, I have corn and wheat inside. It is yours—grind it, make mush of it, cook it anyway you like it. Take all you want."

The oldest of the sisters thanked Tesilya and followed her into the house and set herself to parching corn. She was not shy with her mother-in-law because she knew she was her husband's favorite. Of her he said to his mother, "I knew I should love her before I saw her because I dreamed of her. And she loved me and cared for me when I was bewitched and sick on my way home, and looked like nothing but a bundle of dead, dried cane." And he

[ 125 ]

told his mother that his other wives were this one's younger sisters.

Those others remained outside, standing, ashamed before their mother-in-law, unsure of their welcome. Seeing them so, Tesilya went quickly to them and put out her hands to them leading them inside the house, and saying in her gentle voice, "My daughters-in-law!"

Sun came home, and they talked of many things, on into the night. Ahta-hana told his grandfather and his mother of his journeyings, and Tesilya learned how he had stolen the shinny ball as a beginning toward avenging his father's murder. Now he said he was almost ready to go on with that task. Two things more he needed: good supplies of thunder and of lightning. And his grandfather told him of a pit where they were to be found.

His wives slept, weary from their travels, and while they slept Ahta-hana went swiftly, alone, farther to the east till he came to the pit his grandfather had told him of. His wives were alarmed when they wakened and found him gone, but Tesilya reassured them and comforted them, and, as she had said, he was back home again before night, his arrow case bulging with lengths of hollow cane, each filled with thunder or lightning from the pit. Now, he said, he was ready to meet Hotpa. So the next day, he bid good-bye to Sun and set out over Ahta's and Tesilya's old route westward to the river and the sacred mountain. Tesilya sang a song of farewell to her father and his house, and followed after her son, his four young wives with her.

Word of their coming preceded them. Hotpa and the shinny players stayed close by the sacred mountain, setting up a pole in an open space before their houses and tying Ahta's scalp piece to it. While they sang and danced around the scalp, Hotpa prepared to use the most powerful magic he knew against Ahta-hana.

All the other people came pouring over the desert and across the river. When Ahta-hana and Tesilya reached the river, their relatives and friends were waiting there to give them joyful greeting. Even Ahta's uncle was there. Very old and frail, he did not cry when he saw Tesilya and Ahta-hana; he embraced them, touching their faces and hands again and again, reassuring himself in this way that they were truly come back to him.

When the greetings were over, Ahta-hana left his family and friends where they were on the riverbank. He said that no one was to go with him or to follow after him. Alone, he crossed the river he had come to know so well, and he went close to the dancers and Hotpa. So swiftly and quietly had he come that they only realized he was there when, using his long powerful cane—the one like his father's—as if it were a spear thrower, he threw all of the thunder and lightning he had brought in his arrow case amongst them, causing such a hot and destroying fire that not one of his enemies survived it. Hotpa and the shinny players were consumed in the flames, and every house and article belonging to them was burned down to the ground.

The fire he had started swept out over the desert, and

Ahta-hana was barely able with all his strength and power to stop it at the river's edge. But at last it burned itself out. Ahta's death was avenged, and his people came home to live out their lives within the shadow of the sacred mountain.

Under Ahta-hana's guidance, they followed the way of life which is right for the river people, and continued to dream the dreams which belong to them. Ahta-hana wished his people not to forget their beginnings, nor to lose all memory of their early heroes. To this end he put it into their hearts to be reminded of the good and faithful uncle whenever they heard the soft call of the snowy owl of the Colorado. The river cane of daily use was already, in his time, called by his father's name, and the great red rock by the river's edge would be named for himself when it came time for him to die. As for his wives and his mother, the river people were to see them as the cluster of the Pleiades, Tesilya the brightest star of the tiny constellation. It seemed fitting to her son to think of his mother so, shining softly, high in the winter sky.

Today, the great red rock is called Ahta-hana. The river people smile in remembrance of the old uncle whenever they hear the snowy owl. And they look up often during the clear, dark nights of winter to where the wives of Ahta-hana dance around his mother—the one in the center, the brightest one—Tesilya.

*The Man's Wife*

THE MAN'S wife was a good woman, accomplished in all womanly skills and much beloved by her husband.

One day she died, leaving him bereft and alone, for they were childless. The man had no wish to go on living without his wife. He burned off his hair, smeared his face with mud, and when his wife was buried, refused to leave her grave or to eat or to be in any way consoled. He made a shallow hollow where he lay, his face turned to the grave, and there he stayed crying and blowing tobacco smoke from his pipe over the grave, and repeating from time to time, "I shall wait for you. When you leave, I shall go with you."

For two days and two nights he lay without food or sleep, waiting for his wife. Toward the end of the second night there was a stirring of the loose dirt over her, and she sat up. She did not see her husband, but sat for some time shaking the dirt from her hair, smoothing it with her hands, and tying it back with a narrow band of mink. She cleaned the clinging pieces of dirt from the strands of beads around her neck and over her breasts, then she stood up, straightening her skirt and apron. Clean and neat as in life she stood turning to the north, the south, and the east as if unsure of her directions. Finally she turned to the west, moving slowly away from the grave, westward, without speaking to her husband, still unaware that he was there watching her every motion, and crying.

Following her, the man tried again and again to put his arms around his wife, but he could not hold her; she slipped through his hands. He was, however, able to tie around her slim waist a rope of eagle's down, and clinging to one end of it, he walked a few steps behind her all through the night.

He could see her plainly as long as it was dark, but with daylight she became invisible. He was sure she must be lying across the trail, resting, because the eagledown rope lay there. The old men at home, he remembered, always said that the dead travel only during the dark of the sun. And he felt fairly sure his wife had not escaped him, for the path of the dead was plainly marked, and he could discern his wife's footprints upon it only as far as they had travelled. But as he sat patiently waiting for the sun to set and darkness to come again, keeping his eyes fixed on the trail ahead, he made out there the footprints of many,

many others, and among them he was sure he recognized some which belonged to relatives and to old friends dead a long or a short time.

As day darkened to night there was a pull on the eagle-down rope, and the wife, once more visible, got to her feet and recommenced her journey along the trail, her husband following after as on the night before. Again darkness gave way to light, the second day passing as had the first, the man's wife invisible to him, unmoving; the man holding to the rope as his clue, keeping his eyes on the trail ahead.

During the whole of the journey he neither slept nor took any food. He smoked his pipe from time to time, blowing the smoke toward his wife while he prayed and cried. So passed one like another, four nights and four days.

They were now close to the land of the dead, and as darkness obscured the day for the fourth time and he could again see his wife, she spoke at last. "Why do you follow me so far, my husband?" she said.

"Because I cannot live without you. Where you go, I shall go."

"But that is not possible." Her voice was gentle and familiar. "Go back to the land of the living while you still can find your way. I must go on, but from here it will be difficult and dangerous for you."

But the man answered her, "I mean to bring you away from that land. Or if I cannot, to stay there with you."

"I believe that that cannot be done," she said, and

[ 133 ]

added coaxingly, "Don't you know—I am nothing now. You cannot by any means get my body back. It went from you when I died."

"Others have said that to me. Nonetheless I believe that I can because I so strongly will it," the man said.

His wife was troubled, but she said no more of his turning back. It would be useless to try to persuade him. It must come out as it would.

On and on they went, the trail ever steeper and narrower and rougher. At one place, it skirted a chasm so deep it appeared to be bottomless, and with only shallow footholds hewn in the rock for a crossing. Here she implored her husband to leave her, greatly fearing that he would slip and be hurled to his death. But, as before, he refused. Slowly, carefully, they made their way across the chasm. Not far beyond, the trail was blocked by two enormous boulders in uneasy balance, sliding apart and clashing together with such violence as to crush a person or animal who chanced to be caught between them. They were no real barrier to the man's wife, because her bones were of course left behind in her grave. She passed between them lightly and quickly, and watched with fear while her husband waited for them to slide apart. Hurling himself between them, repeating a prayer and clinging still to the eagledown rope, the man just made it to his wife's side before the rocks crashed together.

And so at last, on the evening of the sixth day, they came to the banks of the swift river which divides the land of the dead from that of the living—a river spanned only by a narrow, swaying bridge made of strands of grass rope.

The guardian of the bridge talked to them, as is his custom, learning who they were and the village from which they came, and telling them of their relatives who had already crossed over to the other side.

He did not try to dissuade the man from going, sensing his determination and his power. He did, however, warn him that even if his prayers and strength of purpose put him across the bridge, the dead would feel it an intrusion to have a living person amongst them.

He warned them that the bridge was treacherous in its erratic swaying and dipping, and that many fell from it into the river, from which there was no chance of rescue and where monstrous fish devoured them. He reminded them also that demon birds would fly up, trying to frighten them so that they would miss their footing and fall.

The man and his wife said they would go on. It was as the guardian said—demon birds flew before and around them filling the air with their loud cries and making even more hazardous the trip over the slippery, unsteady bridge. But they neither listened to them, nor looked down into the swift waters below. They kept their gaze ahead, the man clung to the rope around his wife's waist, and together they arrived on the far shore and stepped off the bridge into the land of the dead.

The chief of that land met them almost as they stepped

from the bridge. To the man's wife he said, "You have come—you bring a companion with you?"

She answered him, "He is my husband. He is a living man."

The chief told her, "I will speak with him. Meanwhile go with my messenger here. He will help you to find your relatives."

When she was gone with the messenger, the chief turned to her husband who was crying, his face distorted and mud-smeared from mourning, and he felt pity for him. He sent him to swim and clean himself; then he had his own daughters bring him food and drink. It had been many days since the man had eaten or drunk, and he accepted the food gratefully. Only after this did the chief question him, asking him how he could have reached this land never before visited by a living person. The man explained how he had come, and the chief said to him, "Tell me, why did you make this dangerous journey?"

"To recover my wife and take her back to the world with me. Or if I cannot do that, to stay here with her."

The chief knew this was a good and strong man, one who, having fasted and prayed, had learned much control and gained much power. He felt he must do for him what he could. He said, speaking carefully, "You should not have come. You are asking for something which we have no power to give you. You must know that we have here only your wife's shadow, that she has left behind in the grave her bones and her body. How can we give these things back to you? You should return to the world and content yourself until it is your time to die.

"Since you are come, and since I believe you to be a good man, you are welcome. But not for long. I must warn you that to the dead the smell of the living is offensive, and there will be a restiveness among them, a feeling of the impropriety of your being here at all. But stay for a little if you will. You will learn how it is with the dead, and that I speak truly. Do not by any means try to steal your wife away. Do not try to sleep with her."

The man sat apart from the dead, quiet, watching. As darkness crept over the land, campfires were lighted one after another until there was a circle of fires all around the open place kept for dancing, and the dead became visible to the man. He recognized his own relatives at one fire, and friends from long ago at another; in the light of still another fire, he saw his wife, surrounded by her own people. He was lonely, but he made no move to join his wife or his relatives, staying where he was and observing the seemingly happy and carefree dead, as they sat by their fires talking or playing the stick game. More and more as the night wore on, they left their fires to dance in the open space the round dance of the dead. He saw that his wife, too, talked, and played the stick game with the women, and that later she also danced. The dancing stopped only with the first dawn, and while the others went off, the man's wife turned back and came to her husband where he sat alone. Because of the daylight he could not see her, but she lay beside him, and they talked together all during the day. When night fell and he could see her, he desired her and tried to fondle her as he was accustomed to do in life, but almost at once he was overcome with sleep. When he wakened, she was gone to play in one of the games and to dance again with the dead.

Again she came to him when dawn began to break, and again she stayed with him, talking to him all day, and he had no thought of sleep. Again he tried to be as a husband to her when it was dark, again he slept, and again she was gone to join the other dead when he wakened.

After all this had happened for the third time, the chief came to the man to tell him that he could stay no longer, that the dead did not feel it to be right to allow a living person to remain among them. But, since he had grieved so deeply and gone through so much to be with his wife, the chief said that she would be allowed to return with him and to her life in the world of the living. He made only one condition: during the trip home, which would take six days and six nights, and until they were home again, the man must not touch his wife.

Joyously the man agreed. The wife, when the chief asked her if she wished to return to her home with her husband, said, "Yes." She knew that this is not how it is between the living and the dead, but she loved her husband, and she could see that he did not know how to live without her.

Together they left the land of the dead, going back across the bridge, between the moving rocks, and over the long trail, on and on until six days and five nights had come and gone and they were once more in country familiar to them. By the next day they would reach their own home.

But as darkness replaced the last of the light from the setting sun at their backs and the man could again see his wife looking quite as she had in life, he could wait no longer. He must and he would have her. She pleaded with him to wait through this one night. He could not. He took her—his love and his longing, his fasting and prayers all given to this moment.

The man's wife vanished, never to return to him.

The sun was high in the sky the next day when hunters from his own village found the man. He was dead, lying face down, arms outstretched, on the trail which leads to the west.

*About the Stories*

# Some Qualities of Indian Stories

THE "oralness" of oral literature is what sets it off from its written descendants in ways which are, some of them, just coming to be appreciated. In place of the written word reacting upon its reader, there is the storyteller retelling a familiar tale. He may tell it without change and embellishment; or expand his material at will; or slur it over, exhibiting not only his individual comprehension of what he is relating, but (in his voice, his gestures, his facial expressions, and in innumerable, tiny, unconscious muscular tensings and untensings) his own emotional reaction to it. And looking at him as well as listening to him, his audience—usually multiple—by its individual and collective reaction determines something of what the storyteller makes of the story, and what its "affect" and ultimately its form will be. This interaction is of both psychological and literary interest. Its literary aspect will become better understood only after specialists in these matters have analyzed the significant, unconscious gesture, described it fully, and weighed the part it plays in interpersonal relations, and hence in art.

Oralness is a goal of much that is written. Songs are to be sung, poetry is to be recited, plays are to be acted, stories are to be read aloud. So is history for that matter: it is only when you *hear* them read that you fully appreciate Gibbon as a stylist, or Plutarch as a storyteller, or Tacitus as a character-izer of nations and people.

Turning the coin over, we know only so much of an old oral body of myth and story as has been preserved in written record, either in phonetic transcription or in translation. From native California, we have a literature cut off in its course be-fore its stylists could impress their genius beyond their own lifetime, before form as we know it could crystallize and emerge. But some configuration becomes apparent as one reads through the recorded material. It contains didactic subjects—history and religion, ethics and etiquette; entertain-ment and some few stories probably intended for children; humor; and the whole creative and "feeling" range in litera-ture. There are tales tender and nostalgic, or bitter and terri-fying, having to do with heroism, love, pride, jealousy, bastardy, incest, and murder.

How we came to relegate such material to juvenilia is an intriguing question. The answer would probably explain how early Greek myths, the *Arabian Nights,* and Gulliver have met somewhat the same fate, recalcitrant as they all are to reduc-tion to fare for children.

Native to California were more than twenty separate peo-ples, differing widely in physique, in customs and beliefs, and

with separate languages which were further differentiated by dialects within the languages. It follows that their arts, including their literatures, also differed. But there are some binding patterns which make a unity within the differences.

Of these, I should put first the *settledness* of these people to whom the golden land once belonged. To none of them was it a frontier. It was the homeland, and nothing could have differed more from the ways and values of a frontier than the boundaried and ancient life they knew, a life unchanged through all remembered generations, unchanged back to the very beginning of the world. Their literary and philosophical and historical assumptions were those which grew out of a world, small, particularized, and static, of known boundaries traversable in a single extended journey, with a sky overhead which was not so far away as to be inaccessible. Knowledge of other, outside worlds was remote and of only remote interest as compared with interest in one's own land, its people and its past.

Their literature must be viewed also against a background of tabu, ritual, and magic, which pervaded the total structure of the society, and of a religion at once mystical and fatalistic and omnipresent, the supernatural and the natural aspects of life interwoven as weft and warp. The overall temperament of the California Indian is unboastful, grave, subtle, and introverted—of a piece as compared with Basin and Plains Indians to the east.

In selecting the nine stories of this collection, I was little concerned to show a wide geographic spread of great variety; my purpose was rather to present a handful of my favorites. But a glance at the map will show that the stories come from the north, the south, the interior, and the coast. And no two are alike. One points toward the novel form, one to the tragic drama. One suggests a morality tale, another a masque fantasy. One prefigures the lyric, one the idyll, and one the epic form. There is a romance and there is an Orpheus-like myth.

I believe that it is not by chance that all but two of my choices are single in origin, and without variants; and that of those two, one, "Loon Woman," belonged to people who were neighbors, and the other, the Orpheus story, belonged in its particularities to only three neighboring peoples of the central valley. My tentative guess is that the budding, creating element in oral literature may well lie within the unique tale, invented by a single person, and tangential to the great, conventionalized, and channeled main stream of a people's literary *corpus* and tradition.

Two further tentative generalizations I would draw from my reading. One is that the devices, patterns, and structure which I find in these brief stories suggest a germinal prefiguring of a written and sophisticated literature. If I am right in this, oral literature can be read to discover whatever it contains of prehistory in the morphology of literature.

My second generalization is that perhaps the culture of a people must have progressed beyond serious insecurity, economic and psychic, and must include considerable leisure and a climate of permissiveness and appreciation, for its spinners of tales to venture much outside the limits of familiar myth and story.

The Yurok-Karok and the Mohave-Yuman are the Indian cultures of California with story styles most removed from the primitive. Both had much more economic leeway than had the peoples living between them, and hence more leisure. The Mohave style developed in a large land, under a democratic and relaxed interpersonal code. The Yurok, quite differently, grew in a small world, amongst a tense people concentrated upon high personal achievement—a value which was an amalgam of an extreme of personal puritanism and personal ambition, and the ideal of a familial aristocracy of birth and wealth.

And now to the stories.

# The Stories in This Book

## 1. THE INLAND WHALE

"THE Inland Whale" is a story told by the Yurok Indians. It shares with "Umai" and "About-the-House Girl" a story style accurate, clear, concise, and with an unusual sense for niceness of exact meaning. The Yurok homeland is along the lower Klamath River, to the sea. Details of geography, ours and Yurok, and of the Yurok world concept, I shall leave to the discussion of "Umai," where they are more particularly relevant.

The Yurok, and the Karok upstream from them, lived differently from their neighbors to the east, on the other side of the coast range, and (as did the Mohave of the great valley of the Colorado in comparison with their near desert neighbors) they lived better. From the Klamath came salmon—all anyone could eat fresh or smoked or dried. From the ocean came sea lions, sea otters, an occasional whale, surf fish, mussels—the wealth of the cold and unpolluted Pacific waters. In the hills behind the ocean and above the river, but never far from either, were elk and deer, and tan oaks for acorns; and lining the canyon walls were redwood trees for canoes and houses.

This small and well-stocked world of the Yurok allowed for the accumulation of wealth, and in their mores wealth was a positive virtue. To possess money—strings of dentalium shells of exactly known value and a customary medium of exchange —to own property, to live in a good house with a name of its own, to be spoken of up and down river and on the coast, oneself and one's family, as people of substance and virtue, this was good. To have handed down to one, and in turn to hand on to one's son, the ceremonial flints and obsidian knives of great antiquity and sacredness, to own cylindrical wooden chests full of the incredibly sumptuous featherwork regalia used in ritual dances, perhaps to own a rare white deerskin, these were good things.

The ideal and bent of the culture was aristocratic. While it was of course desirable to acquire as much as one could of goods and money, it was better to begin from a platform than from the ground. Wealth tended to be kept in a family, to descend from father to son to grandson. It was also good to marry well, to choose one's wife for her virtue and good looks, and from as well-regarded and wealthy a family as could be managed. And so one paid the father of one's bride with money and gifts, and the more one paid the more honor accrued to bride and groom and their families.

With aristocracy and wealth went puritanism and an elaborate code of allowed deportment. Wealth was not come by nor kept unless one prayed as well as worked, observed correct ritual and secular behavior toward the gods and one's fellows, restrained the impulse to greed in eating or to any other coarsenesses, to laziness or any laxness, to indulgence in sex.

By a happy chance "The Inland Whale" was told to me before I or anyone else had recorded it, and under circumstances in which the telling was as nearly spontaneous and full as is possible for a Yurok speaking in English to a non-Yurok.

Robert Spott told me the story. I realize only now, writing this, that, well as we knew Robert, I cannot give you his Yurok name. The matter of the personal name is one that is left in abeyance unless its owner chooses to tell it, and Robert, so far as I remember, did not ever do so. He belonged to one of the best families along the river. His looks, his bearing, his manners, remained benevolently aristocratic and his devotion to Yurok values undeviating, despite the almost total breakdown of his own culture, and despite his participation in the world of today. He went to school, he won a personal citation from the French Government in the first World War, he was the foreman of a road-building crew in Humboldt County, he was spokesman for the Yurok in dealings with government or sportsmen, all of whom claimed river rights, and all of whom trusted Robert.

He owned his own home, a small, immaculately kept house in Rekwoi, with a terrace like that of Pekwoi, except that it was not stone paved. From this terrace he looked steeply down onto the mouth of the Klamath River and out over the ocean. His "aunt," Fanny Flounder, the last of a Yurok line of famous doctors, lived nearby in a house similar to Robert's. She and I were sitting on her terrace in the sun one day and looking down at the river which had only just broken itself a new opening through the bar. Fanny watched intently as the surf from an incoming tide seemed to push back the river and to overspread the wide river mouth. "You see there what is wrong with the world," Fanny said to me, pointing to the break-through. "The earth tips too far and the ocean comes up the river. That is not good. Even whales could come into the river when it is this way. It happens because there are not enough Yurok anymore; not enough people dancing and stamping their feet down hard on the earth. That is what used to keep it from tipping, and what kept whales outside where they belong."

The day Robert first mentioned anything of an inland whale, he was with us in the Napa Valley. He had finished smoothing and leveling a circle about ten feet in diameter on the rough hillside by our house, and building a wall of stone breast high to enclose the eastern or "land" side of the circle. St. John's Mountain, the Valley of the Moon, and a low coast range intervene between the Napa Valley and the sea, but he had nonetheless made sure that the seaward facing direction of the wall for what we regarded as an outdoor fireplace was as it should be for a *tsektseya*, or altar as one might call it. Robert's *tsektseya* exquisitely symbolized the Yurok view as contrasted with our own. For us, he had made a concave wall of stone within which a large outdoor fire could be safely burned in California's rainless and dry grass summers, leaving a half circle for sitting around it, warm and sheltered from the night down-canyon draft.

Robert's view was, you might say, inside out. For, used as a *tsektseya*, a person would sit within and against the encircling walls, introvertedly sheltered and alone, looking toward the open sea. The Yurok have numbers of such structures in their own hills above the river at particular spots reserved for them since time immemorial. They are places of retreat for a man or a woman who, seeking power, goes to them to pray, to cry, to smoke, to fast: in short to engage in ceremonial lonely ritual, these being places of solitary mystic communion. They are good places, Robert said, to sit and listen to the songs of the different birds, learning from them to throw the voice high in the strangely frenetic falsetto singing which accompanies the sacred dances. More important of course, they are where one hopes to hear the distant Spirits who may listen and take pity on the one praying there, a place for gathering one's resources in many ways.

Robert was pleased to have built a *tsektsoya* so far from home, and, since his Yurok world was immanent wherever he was, he was reminded of those altars at home where he had prayed and fasted, and of others which he had found abandoned and fallen apart. From this there followed anecdotes of one person and another, among them a man who was poor and without family, in fact, a bastard. Such a one, plainly, was of low caste and would in all probability remain so, but again, perhaps not. There was always the inland whale. Robert's English, like his inner orientation, remained grounded in Yurok, but he had a nice sense for the precise. He explained, "When I was fifteen years old, my father told me of the inland whale, and I learned from him that I must always be compassionate of bastards." Then came the magic beginning words, "After the waters which covered the world went down . . ." and the story followed, told with clarity and passion, a Yurok phrase or a Wogè prayer weaving in and out without self-consciousness or interruption.

[ 153 ]

As I listened, it came to me that I was being treated to an oral precursor of the novel.

It is necessary to be quite specific as to what I mean by this. I do not mean that one afternoon, by chance, I discovered *the* seedling novel in a literature without writing and, so far as we understand it, without "true" or developed poetry.

Poetry seems always to have preceded the novel. We know how heavily epic and narrative poetry have contributed to the western novel. The Chinese and Japanese did not have epic poetry, but the Japanese had history, romanticized history, done in a rhythmic *recitatif,* and the Chinese had lyric poetry which included realistic, domestic elements, before their earliest novels. The novel is a late and complex configuration, impure in the sense that earlier forms lie half-concealed within it, and that it lacks the definition of any of these others. One is reminded of the operá, which is also impure, borrowing and adapting from drama, song, and dance, more fluid and less defined than any of the three.

It has followed that no two critics agree in all particulars as to what is and what is not a novel. Is *Eugene Onegin* a novel, though poetry? Is Madame de La Fayette's *La Princesse de Clèves* a novel, or a romance? But within the differences there are agreements. The time span may vary to cover one life, or generations, or to be contained within the rising and setting of a single sun. A novel is fictional, a work of the imagination, but, properly speaking, realistic: it "could be." Its people could be actual people, the words put into their mouths could have been said, the events of the story could have taken place. Its *locus* is, more often than not, one in the real world, either so designated or thinly disguised or generalized; or, if imaginary, again within the realms of the "could be." A novel is longer than a novella or short story, but is more especially distinguished from them in that it explores more widely or more deeply. It is presumed to be born of moral conviction and hence to have scope sufficient to compensate for its sacrifice of the elegance of precise structure.

So, when I say that "The Inland Whale" appears to me to be a precursor of the novel, I am speaking of its structure and scope and the focus of its story. It is of skeletal brevity but the sort of frame upon which novels have been hung. For, swiftly told, bare and concise as is the tale, it encompasses the history of a house, its pride, its decay, its restoration, through four generations of the family which peopled it.

And it is realistic, although embedded in ancient Wogè belief, and despite the inland whale herself. Mystic belief, even miracles, and surely the sense of awe and divinity can belong in a novel, to be understood literally if one so believes, or symbolically if one prefers. The inland whale is no more demanding in this regard than *Kuan-Yin* or the Virgin Mary, both of whom she resembles in her pity for the unfortunate and low-born.

The story is laid in *Ko'otep*, anglicized as Kotep, once an actual village on the Klamath River. *Pekwoi* is the name of a real house, now fallen in with only its pit left. The graveyard by the river, Robert said, is now merely a bare grassy place, but its location is exactly known. The journey undertaken by the young mother of the story is accomplished as such a journey on foot would be today (see the map accompanying the story): by trail from *Ko'otep*, skirting the river to the spot on Camp Creek where the Deerskin Dance was held. The return follows the same trail as far as Red Cap Creek; then inland away from the river, passing alongside Fish Lake and by

[ 155 ]

*Kewet* Mountain, thus bypassing the populous village of *Weit-spus*, coming out on the river again at *Murek*, and from there on downstream to *Ko'otep* once more.

The distances from place to place could be travelled on foot in the time the story allots them. All this is in interesting contrast to "Umai," the other Yurok story, in which distances and time are treated idyllically, consonant with Wogè, not human, conceptions and capacity.

On the other hand, the story is fiction. It pretends to be the story of the family that really lived in the house *Pekwoi*. *Pekwoi* has not been occupied for a long time, however, and no one can now relate its former owners to living Yurok. The story gives to it the sort of family which would have occupied such a house, and tells what might well have befallen its members. There is also the ideal, the wish fulfillment, the rags to riches aspect of the story. Given the Yurok inheritance pattern, and the rarity of the objects of great worth, and the difficulty of acquiring wealth when starting from nothing, it is improbable that in real life Toàn the hero, could have accomplished all that he does in the story.

His achievement remains within the possible, however, and the way he brings it to pass, and his deportment—even to returning at long last to the ancestral home—are kept within the bounds of realistic and probable behavior. No one at any time in the story does anything fanciful, fantastical, or unreal. No one is given a character that sits unnaturally upon him; no one acts other than believably, or expresses himself in any way incompatible with the nature he has been given.

The story can be read in depth microcosmically, its delicate clues leading down and down into the Yurok psyche; and macrocosmically, its nostalgia and its passion being also quite simply human. I know of no other story from the California Indians in which the treatment of character and material so strongly suggests the novelistic approach. Always rare in folklore, this approach is one which has a way of rising to the top in collections of favorites. (Look at the Lang and Björnsen collections.) Any extensive collection of folklore, any discussion with someone who has recorded and collected in Africa, Oceania, Asia, or Europe, bears testimony to such occasional novelistic treatment of material the world over. This suggests that the characteristic techniques of the novel are older than is commonly assumed in discussions of its history and origins. Not as old as songs and lullabies and prayers, nor as the stories of creation and custom and belief, but old.

Once a people has satisfied its need for these primal literary modes, and if there are stability and an audience ready for introduction to something more sophisticated, and more individual, the creative imagination begins, apparently, to play with form, and poetry or organization akin to poetry emerges; and to play with content, with the actual human condition, to memorialize it in fictional, realistic, narrative dramatization. And that this should be so is heartening. For the artist as novelist is artist as "human-ist," his ideal the celebration of living, erring, struggling, achieving man. It is good to realize that the impulse to give expression to this may be as old as the first time man looked upon his fellow men, not in fear or in need, but with inner security and objectivity sufficient that he could feel toward them curiosity and compassion.

## 2. LOON WOMAN

"Loon Woman" is a terrifying and portentous tale of a sister who, in love with one of her brothers, publicly forces him to go away with her and brings disaster to herself and to her family. It has been found among eight different peoples, geographically contiguous in interior northern California: the Modoc, Yana, Shasta, Achomawi, Atsugewi, Maidu, Karok, and Wintu.

Incest is the core of the story and its universal aspect which relates it to all peoples and all times. Humankind constitute but a single species, but for all their biological and genetic uniformity, peoples have proliferated so variously in their cultures that there remain only a few traits which can with confidence and apparent truth be called universals. One of these few is prohibition of sexual intercourse between father and daughter, mother and son, or between brother and sister. Such a relation has been regarded by all peoples at all times as incestuous and abhorrent no matter how differently and variously blood relation beyond the nuclear family has been construed. The apparent exceptions, the enjoining to marriage of a brother and sister of the blood royal, or at the time of creation to begin the peopling of the world, give subtle emphasis to the universal norm by their rarity and specialness. Many of the creation myths which rely upon this device for populating the world, specify predecessors of modern man who are either different from him, half-gods or animal gods or immortals like the Wogè of the Yurok and the Ikharéya of the Karok.

The strong social pressure against the incestuous relation, and the ever recurrent impulse to it, have been the subject of oral and written literature over and over again. Its dramati-

[ 158 ]

zation served Greece's greatest tragedians so well that it not only became the subject of some of their most enduring plays but carried over into the modern diagnostic vocabulary of psychoanalysis. It continues to reappear in all stages of literature including the present—witness William Faulkner for example, or the poet Robinson Jeffers. And it turns up again and again in native Indian myth, all over North America.

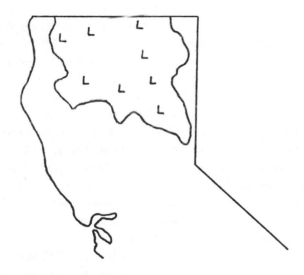

But nowhere outside its own limited boundaries does any story resemble "Loon Woman." The story comes to us uneasy in the relation of its parts, a jig-saw puzzle, only partially assembled, of pieces old and new, some intrinsic to it, some belonging to other story configurations. There are extant not more than fifteen recorded versions, one never quite like another. All have the core of the story, but those pieces which would

[ 159 ]

have come to inhere to the core, given more organization and a fuller molding, are sometimes present, sometimes missing. Nor had the paring away of extrinsic episodes been seriously begun. The interrupted and half-finished state demonstrates one sort of story formation actually in process—much as the archeologist sees in the roughly shaped pot in the hands of the potter struck down at his task, and in the wares set out for sale or barter, how the ancient Pompeiian shaped a pot, and what his wife took home from market.

It is not possible to say what the age of the "Loon Woman" story is. Curtin was the first to record it, a Modoc version, around 1893. It was as formed, and as unformed, then as when Dr. Demetracopoulou recorded it from the Wintu in 1929. This was to be expected: its cultural and story milieu was pretty much shattered before 1893. It may well have been a "young" story. I like to think of it as in a formative stage.

Formative, in a sense, it certainly is, but it need not also have been newly made. It has an ambitious plot. Storytellers must have differed in their capacity to handle it and audiences in their reactions to it and their preferences as to how it should be told. Some versions have a second part which I do not retell, or analyze here. Occasionally this part is long and much elaborated, explaining how, after Loon Woman's death, her parents and brothers are magically restored to life. The added part is in another emotional key, and its inclusion suggests constraint and a possible wobbliness in handling the difficult material of Loon Woman's own story. The added part returns teller and listener to concepts familiar and undemanding.

Nor can one with any certainty infer age from distribution. Dispersal over a wide area is at least presumptive evidence of age, but limitation of area is not nearly as good evidence of recentness. "Loon Woman" may well have had only limited appeal. The Karok version from which I borrow Loon Woman's name, *Ishanihura*, as well as her brother's name, *Makikirèn*, and the episode of the macabre dance and song of Ishanihura at the fire which was consuming the bodies of her family, did not include the bringing back to life, which is not surprising. But neither does the Karok version have the distinctive, eerie abnormality of mood and character adhering to the story in the area of its fullest realization. The Karok may have found it not to their taste; certainly they were competent to handle it had they so wished.

There are only about ten story elements in "Loon Woman," and all but three of these are familiar in other contexts and areas, yet there clings to her story an aura of the special and unique. The familiar discrete events tend to take on a changed significance, to have been given a twist which alters their connotation. This is true for the brother-sister incest theme. There are brother-sister incest stories from all over North America, sometimes to account for the peopling of the world, sometimes as part of the Coyote-Trickster sort of outlandish behavior, sometimes, as in "Loon Woman," with awareness of perversity and a fear born of this awareness. But Ishanihura, the Loon Woman, guards with *secrecy* her guilty feelings and plans, and this new factor of secrecy changes the story from one of moral disapproval and some fear, to one of sheer terror. Also, Ishanihura overrides all efforts to control or divert her, publicly forcing her brother to accompany her as would a husband, and this *public* insistence is unheard of in other tales; indeed it is almost out of the experience of its narrators to imagine even in mythic behavior.

[ 161 ]

Revenge for a wrong done is, of course, an old theme; the particular form of the revenge on Ishanihura remains peculiar to this story except that the old Achilles heel motif is used unchanged. In some versions, the revenge episode, like the added part of the bringing back to life of the hearts of Loon Woman's family, is elaborated into magic and myth of familiar emotional limits, and again it would seem that the narrator is escaping depths too deep for him or his listeners. But the revenge which is the preferred one, and which accords best with the story, is a brief and circumstantial shooting with an arrow in the vital part, as Dr. Demetracopoulou says, much as an actual loon is shot and its body recovered from the water.

The hiding away from the world of a beautiful child, whether the eldest or the youngest, and I believe always a son, is an old motif and a favorite one on the Northwest Coast, among other places. I have the impression that, since this is accomplished differently in each version, and remains one of the least limpid of the elements in the story, that the narrators of "Loon Woman" had not settled upon an implicit meaning for it in their own minds.

Another of the elements widespread in North America is that of the substitution of a log for a person. It is subtilized sometimes as in "Loon Woman" by making the log a piece of old alder that is of no more weight than that of a man, and by using a forked piece. In "Loon Woman" the brother substitutes the alder for himself in order that he may escape his sister, who has become fearful to him. It is the association of log substitution and *fearfulness* that is unique to this particular story. It is only the turn of the screw from joke or convenience to terror, but it is a turn which makes all the difference.

The flight-to-the-sky motif would be expected to occur wherever the sky is understood to be a habitable part of the world and within reach, and so it does. But it is only in "Loon Woman" and in one other Shasta story in the center of the loon-story area that disaster follows from looking down while *ascending* to the sky. Elsewhere, and logically enough the prohibition is against looking down while descending. Again an old concept is given a new twist.

Hurrying the sun is not a widely dispersed element. The Washo have it as do the Modoc, but it is only within the loon-woman area that the hurrying is done for *amorous reasons*.

So much for the elements found in other places and other tales. The all-important incident of the finding of the single hair with the current of following events; the killing of Loon Woman, that is to say, the specific revenge; and the explanation of the white band of feathers which encircles a loon's neck as a necklace of human hearts—these are the three elements which were invented for "Loon Woman" and do not occur otherwise. And they are the crucial elements.

The motif of a single hair floating on the water and coming to the attention of a young girl who measures it and finds it to be exactly the length of her own and who then fixes on the hair as a symbol of the desired lover leads ever so quietly to the dark, turbulent depths of the drama to follow.

The second invention, the necklace of human hearts, the hearts of her own father and mother and brothers which Ishanihura strings around her neck, sufficiently sums up the intervening horror and passion and violence, and forecasts retributive punishment before there can be a final ending to the tragedy.

Klytemnestra showed an equal violence, but Klytemnestra was a woman wronged. There is rather something Dostoevskian in the sheer audacity and psychopathology of the evil which possessed Ishanihura. That the stark story woven of the single hair and the heart necklace was beyond the imaginative sophistication of the peoples of its origin does seem strongly probable in view of the length and detail of the added parts which, unlike the story proper, are at a level consonant with the run of their other recorded myths and tales.

Nor is this saying more than that the originators, probably the Wintu, once had in their midst an imaginative artist who was appreciated if not wholly understood. His people did what they could with the story he created; and they passed it along to their neighbors.

It is a powerful story, strikingly imaginative. It invites comparison with the Greek tragic sense. It sets one to reviewing the dramatic motifs and devices of the Greek myths, upon which a curious difference emerges. The Greeks were as interested in dramatizing the terrible and far-reaching effects of incest as were the Indians of North America. But, whereas in native America it was usually brother-sister incest, in Greek myth it was father-daughter, mother-son incest. I have no theory as to what this means. Its interest is probably more directly psychological than literary; it must surely indicate something of the orientation and "set" of the cultures. I regret that I can offer the observation here only as a cultural *curiosum*.

"Loon Woman," in my judgment, is the story from native California which most strongly suggests the tragic drama both in subject matter and in style. Its realism is too drastic, its passion too explosive for another medium than that of the stage tragedy.

## 3. BUTTERFLY MAN

"BUTTERFLY Man" is a tale which, like "Dance Mad," comes single and unimitated in a literature for the most part heavily influenced by surrounding peoples and containing bits and pieces from beyond the barrier of the Sierras to the east, and from as far away as the Pacific coast to the west, with interchange between the nearby Wintu, Yana, and Washo.

The story was recorded by Dr. Roland Dixon sometime before 1902 in the course of a series of linguistic and ethnological trips to the Maidu, whose home is in northeastern California in the valley and hills between the Sacramento River and the Sierras and cut through by the Feather River.

"Butterfly Man" is a cautionary tale. It has the brevity, the barrenness, the inevitable retribution for wrongdoing which are the properties of cautionary tales wherever they are found. They also have a way of being pan-human.

It has always been my suspicion that the cautionary tale which survives does so for reasons other than its moral, which, if the story be interesting, is taken in stride: the coda, as it were, proper to the form.

Dr. Dixon gives no hint as to what "Butterfly Man" may have meant to the Maidu. So far as we know, he recorded it as it came along with Coyote stories, and the "Cannibal Head" story which has travelled rather widely. He gives no indication that he felt it to be at all special.

One can infer an aspect of the Maidu feeling for it in the use of the designation, "Tolowim-Woman." I searched maps and documents, unable to find the whereabouts of the Tolowim, only to learn at last that there are no Tolowim; that so far as is known there never were any Tolowim. With Maidu, we are in a neglected region, linguistically speaking, so that precisely who or what may have been meant it seems impossible at this distance to say. (As I write this, the Maidu language is under study in the Linguistics Department of the University of California.) Perhaps a woman upriver was meant, or downriver, somewhere outside the Maidu world in any case; and she was a bad woman. Probably it was felt that even a bad Maidu woman would never be *that* bad.

All of which is of psychological interest, and encourages me to make a brief *excursus* into the possible origin of the story.

I suggest that it may be a story created from the daydreaming of a Maidu woman. There is first of all the name of the woman, which is that of an outsider, thus clearing the teller, if she is a woman, as well as all other Maidu women, of being like the woefully delinquent one of the story—a matter more important to a woman than to a man. But what I am really thinking of is the imagery.

All up and down California, it was the woman who went into the hills, often with a baby strapped to her back, to gather the seeds and berries and fruits and nuts and ferns and grasses of a hundred uses. Some of them were eaten, some made into clothes or ornaments for skirts and aprons, or dyes for face and body paint; others went to the making of baskets with their patterns woven in grasses of contrasting colors. It was the woman who knew where the best of these crops grew and when they would be ready for gathering. It meant that she spent endless hours in the hills filling her baskets.

And so it would be a woman, crouching over her gathering and picking and digging, or resting in between, who would be sure to have seen more than once this phenomenon of springtime—a hillside, a canyon, a valley filled with countless butterflies of all sizes and colors, flying, hovering, shimmering in the hot sun. I do not know if this butterfly pageant is peculiar to particular places. I have seen it in a fold of hills in the Napa Valley on a sunny April day.

And the fantasy of the butterfly as man in disguise would seem to me a woman's fantasy. The markings suggest easily enough the pattern of headband and breechclout, and the worm body and greedy mouth of the earlier caterpillar form remain in the butterfly, suggesting a rapaciousness and sexuality underlying the gaudy, fluttering wing display.

To conjure up a beautiful man from the strong patterning and coloring of wings; to dream of following him, of leaving to other backs the burden of the cradleboard; to somehow know that the butterfly man, like all men, would be exclusive and unsharing; to envisage a heady time when not one but many butterfly men would desire one: it all seems totally feminine.

That the Tolowim-Woman's story lives on amidst literary company strange to it may be because it continues to remind Maidu women of lonely excursions into the hills, of private daydreams of their own, of a butterfly-filled land.

The reverie dissolves as it must to a woman's way of thinking and feeling. Having sat and in her mind followed her butterfly man, she has had her fun. It is time to take up the cradleboard and go home. No woman who could leave her baby alone for long would come to anything but a bad end, of course. But, there is no need for the end to be too brutal to Tolowim-Woman. It is sufficient that her heart should go away.

## 4. DANCE MAD

"DANCE Mad," light, tripping, its periods marked by the beat of dancing feet, carries a mood rare in the literature of California, and, I should hazard, in most oral literatures.

The recited tale of the "high and far-off times" lends itself to the dignified discursive rhythm of prose epic style and of history, building slowly, architectonically, block of leisurely episode on block of careful detail. If the teller of the tale is thoughtful and of good memory, the cement which holds his blocks together will be that of cultural explication; if he is also an artist in his craft, he will probably indicate as well the cosmological significance of the whole.

And when the tales are not in the grand manner, they will be of another *genre* altogether, most usually that of the trickster. Trickster themes are true "folk" themes. They may explain the blackness of the crow, or why the skunk is striped, or any one of hundreds of other phenomena, natural and supernatural. Something always happens in these stories. Action is intrinsic to their pattern, while motivation need not be appropriate or adequate or consistent; the goodness and the badness of Coyote, or whoever the trickster is, vary from story to story, from mood to mood. These are stories generously salted with the sadistic humor of outwitting and humiliating, and with scatological and erotic humor. The trickster stories are ubiquitous—almost anyone can oblige with a new tale or two.

But there are also stories which are not epic or trickster, whose movement and direction differ from both. These are the odd and probably unique tales that find their way sporadically and unpredictably into literature; these are the stories the ethnologist or folklorist could not have expected to be told, and he could have no formula by which to ask for them. The best storyteller, or let us say the one with the greatest pride and sense of responsibility, will wish, as will the ethnologist, to record first the ancestral myth of a people whose culture is shrinking and giving ground to other ways and other myths. But—this done—if there is time left, and leisure, he may recall a story he has always liked for itself. "Umai," "Butterfly Man," "The Inland Whale," "Dance Mad," "Love Charm," and "About-the-House Girl," of this collection, are such stories. Otherwise unlike, they share the quality of singleness and uniqueness; they are not in any of the travelling, diffusing motif-complexes; they belong to one people only. They are differently organized from other stories, suggesting that they have not "grown," but are rather the creation of a single imagination, close enough to the aesthetic of their culture to have "taken on" and become incorporated into the variety of remembered oral materials, with implicit recognition of their finishedness. One cannot of course say this must have been how it was with them: there is no carbon fourteen proof and no statistical demonstration. They do stand apart *vis à vis* the mythic and diffused and changing tales as singular, as works of art.

"Dance Mad" is a pastoral of the seasons, born of soft air, warm sun, and new green clover, and celebrating the springtime of the earth and of girl-become-woman. Stravinsky's "Rites of Spring" grows out of a primitive, earth-renewing myth of blood sacrifice from the Russian steppes. "Dance Mad" grows out of the Wintu configuration of ritual and psychological and real-life significance centered on a girl's coming of age. This is the crucial experience of a Wintu woman's life. How her family prepare her and themselves for it and how she responds to it will reflect pretty much her adult life experience: her behavior before marriage, particularly toward suitors and possibly lovers; how well and whom she will marry; what sort of wife and mother and grandmother and old woman she will be.

In the story, the fantasy of the dance around the world is an imaginative projection of the actual Wintu feast and dance celebration of the coming of age of a well-born daughter whose family rounds off her completed ritual preparation for womanhood with a general invitation to friends to feast and dance in her honor.

Such a feast and dance could not have been held for Tesilya because her people, the Mohave, attach far less ritual importance, far less *tabu* to a girl's age and maturation, and put less stress than do the Wintu and many others on the unwilled power with which a woman's menses endow her. Where this belief has a strong hold a woman, so long as blood is upon her, may merely by her defiling presence undo a cure a doctor is effecting, or spoil the luck of her husband, or perhaps of a whole village, in war or hunting or gambling.

On the other hand, she has her day of glory as the Mohave woman does not. As "Dance Mad" relates, Nomtaimet, her initiation over, emerges to be made much of. Her beauty is remarked upon; the young matrons treat her graciously; her father gives a feast and dance for her; eligible young men of her village and other villages are aware of her as never before.

But the belief that a woman is dangerous for the period of her menses, until she is no longer able to bear children, takes from her the full human choice to be or not to be good or evil, and to the extent of the limitation on her the belief is surely primitive. It is—at least in California—among peoples backward and underdeveloped as compared with their peers that the fears and *tabus* attaching to the menses become full blown, and include even the Medusa-like covering of the head and face to stay the power for disaster contained in a single glance.

One might expect tensions and release from tensions arising from the restrictive and demanding code to show up in the literature. All there is, however, is an occasional story of the evil resulting from failure to abide by the pattern. Some versions of the "Cannibal Head" story contain this moral, as do some of the versions of "Loon Woman." But both stories ranged over other territory and amongst peoples of greater sophistication than the Wintu, who were by and large more recipient than originating, and had not yet the articulateness nor the story style to take a strong tension in a woman and make of it a full story. That approach might well have had to wait for the beginnings of doubt toward the desirability of the restrictive belief itself. An extremely talented Wintu could —and did—elaborate the creation myth, carrying farther its philosophical implications and its organization. He could not have conceived "The Inland Whale," his culture lacking the self-awareness requisite to envisaging such a story situation.

What the Wintu story style could and did do to admiration was to elucidate and elaborate the bright side of the rite: its

[ 171 ]

resolution of tension. "Dance Mad" is the only story of my nine which has a single and unshadowed mood of gaiety from beginning to end, and gaiety is an exceedingly rare quality in oral literature. The Wintu style of recitation was perfectly suited to such a mood.

"Loknorharas," the source story for "Dance Mad," was not recorded in text, and to give something of the peculiar story style of the Wintu, I will quote from two other stories in the same volume which were taken in text and then translated by Dr. Dorothy Demetracopoulou. "Yiyehunenes' Big Time" begins: "Right there at Redding lived some people. They were going to call a dance. Those that lived there came together right there in the evening. They came together and conferred. They conferred five nights, they conferred five days. They conferred five more nights, they conferred five more days. . . . So they invited, they invited all the world; they invited to a dance, they invited to gambling, they invited to a foot race, they invited to a jumping race, they invited to a round dance, they invited to a beauty contest, they invited all the people. So all who had been invited arrived, kept arriving all night long, arrived all day long, the people who had been invited."

And one of the Wintu accounts of "Loon Woman" begins: "Many people came into being. There was a couple who had many children, nine boys, one girl, ten children. . . . They lived there, and lived there, and lived there, and soon some of their children walked around, some played. The girl lived there, grew up into a woman, and then one morning she went down to the stream, she went to the place where they got water, she sat down, that woman." A dance trip around the world and through the seasons is subject matter appropriate to this staccato, repetitive rhythm, to a style at once so like ballad and ballet. As with lyric poetry, the style is untranslatable in the sense that it becomes quickly monotonous to our ears.

"Dance Mad" is a story born of a gentle people. In stories or actual accounts from other peoples, when dancing takes over after feasting and sociability and excitement, the disruption of the monotonous routine of life, the breaking through puritanical behavior barriers, lead to orgiastic expression—sometimes in real life, more often perhaps in a story account which becomes imagined orgy, or wish fulfillment.

But the dancers in "Dance Mad" break routine drastically without ever departing from the first gentleness of mood. Clothes are shed, but bodies are painted. A sort of choral formality is never lost. The circling of the earth is accomplished as a chorus might dance around the perimeter of a dance plaza or stage, with stops at set intervals for a special dance, for ritual resting, hunting and fishing. The supposed route can be followed on a map of the area traversed in the dance, but it is nonetheless an abstraction of geography. The three rivers do of course come together; the Sacramento River does empty into the ocean. But the order of the dancing is rather that of choreography than geography, the hills, the rivers, and the ocean shore belonging more to fantasy than to topography.

## 5. LOVE CHARM

"THE Love Charm" is a spell said by a Yana girl to bring her beloved to her and to keep him faithful.

The Yana were neighbors of the Wintu and the Maidu in

interior northern California. They lived near streams which arise on the eastern slope of Mt. Lassen and flow into the Sacramento River, in country hilly, tumbled, and forested with brush land opening out from the trees. It is little changed today from its native contour and use; there is an abundance of fish and game now as then, and the serene whiteness of Mount Shasta is still the dominating presence in the land.

My source for the charm is "Spell Said By a Girl Desirous of Getting a Husband," from Dr. Sapir, who recorded and published it in text with interlinear translation followed by an unelaborated Englishing of the text.

"The Love Charm" almost explains itself—not quite—in literal transcription, which goes like this:

"S'uwa!/ May you think about me to yourself!/ May you turn back to look!/ Would that I might stand his/ his/ eye-place!/ I just cry to myself. Would that I might/ see him/ every day! 'I do/ the/ your doing,'/ one who has dreamt/ I do thus/ and I get up/ when it is daylight/ and I/ look about/. Now/ it flutters the/ my heart/ my seeing him/. I look at him slantwise. He gives me/ the/ trinkets and I/ take them/ and I/ for long time/ wear them until worn out. cho!"

In the original, it is the one who pronounces the spell who speaks throughout, sometimes descriptively of herself and her feelings, sometimes saying a phrase or line of the spell. I have put the "setting" in the third person for clarity's sake, and have changed the order to make explicit the separation of the spell itself from the feelings of the speaker. For, to a non-Yana, the seeming simplicity is belied, much as in a Chinese poem, by references and meanings which are implicit and must remain only imperfectly known to the outsider.

To explain it would mean to explain the culture and customs of the Yana, and the charm seems too fragile, too instantaneous, and too tender to need such heavy analysis. Let me say only that it would take the courage of love to drive a Yana girl out, alone, to wait beside a trail for the passing of the one she loves. It was ordinarily "not done," and when she does go, early in the morning to be sure not to miss him, and when he finally comes by, she is too shy to look at him, to let him see her reason for being there. The gifts he makes her would indicate some shyness also on the part of the man—they are not the gestures of experience in love. The "trinkets" would be a flower or a sweetgrass bracelet—perishable and of no value except symbolically.

"The Love Charm" seems to be pre-lyric in form, full lyric in all but form, speaking with poetic sensibility in a single voice, and in the present tense. It is the poetic vehicle of a personal emotion, poignant, restrained, and intense.

## 6. UMAI

WITH "Umai," whose full name is *Mer'wermeris uma'i* or Upriver Ocean Girl—the name of the story as it is told by the Yurok—we move geographically back to the Klamath River, upriver as far as Bluff Creek, downriver to the coast, and for a distance north and south of the river's mouth on the coast. (See end-paper map.) This is a dramatic change from the enclosed interior landscape of the Yana, Wintu, and Maidu peoples to one with the roar of surf breaking on rocky headlands and over big and little sea stacks close to shore; to a wide expanse of sea sometimes fog-enwrapped and wind-blown, sometimes indigo and smooth under a bright sun; to shore lagoons fresh and salt; to a swift river running between canyon walls, making its way to the sea through an ever-shifting sandbar thrown up by the surf against it; to a way of life predicated physically on getting from place to place by canoe—the heavy redwood dugout, strong enough to ride over the rapids and through the surf.

As was to be expected, the literature turns out to be different, too, from that of the interior; some of the difference comes out in the longer stories from this area, "The Inland Whale" and "About-the-House Girl." But in "Umai," short and inconsequential as the story seems, the contrast is already plain.

Yurok and Mohave are alike in their accuracy of geographic fact. The place vagueness of "Dance Mad" would be intolerable to both. Nor would they use the unit number *four* in one story, and *five* in another, as do the Wintu. Such narrative invention is foreign to them, as is any vagueness of *number*. With the Mohave the unit number is always four; with the Yurok, five or ten. What the Yurok and Mohave share in their story style, to put it more generally, is accuracy and definition in the way phenomena are regarded, and hence reported.

For the rest, their literature could not be more unlike, nor could their appearance and temperament: the Mohave with his relatively heavy frame and almost slouching walk, his broad generously smiling face, the relaxation in his sex attitude, his wide wandering, pushing beyond frontiers into strange territory, luxuriating in laziness as in periodic war and work; the Yurok, small-boned and slender, moving with a highbred elegance, proud, aristocratic, tense, contentious, puritanical, demanding much of himself and of others, ever aware of class and caste and decorum, legalistic, and preferring not to leave his own well-known world, preferring for the most part not to think about worlds beyond his own.

One may regard the Mohave as a far northern thrust of the complex and urban civilizations of ancient Mexico, and the Yurok as a southernmost outpost of the high Northwest Coast culture—this is respectable anthropological canon. Whatever the antecedent causes and histories, their literatures suggest the possibility that their clarity and definition may be linked to a way of life, generous in its physical make-up, and with a sufficiently developed individuation and sophistication to have released the human imagination from the primitive amorphousness of the myths and fears and beliefs which underlie the generic "Indian" psyche; which have always underlain in slightly differing specificities the generic human psyche.

Now, once there is this release, the artist is free to play up, and not down, the idiosyncrasies of his milieu and culture and particularized vision, as "Umai" almost perfectly demonstrates. For "Umai" is saturated with the assumptions peculiar to the Yurok, beginning with its being set in Wogè times, and including such matters as the size of the earth and the physical disposition of sky and oceans, as well as the feeling-tone and mood.

Who are the Wogè? The Wogè are people of the golden age of the world, half-gods, immortals, whose knowledge and wisdom and labors made all things ready for the Yurok who should follow them. The nostalgia which pervades the Yurok personality as the sea fog does their coast was present already in the Wogè. They too loved the world and looked forward sadly to having to leave it. The Wogè live on in loving memory, as the prayer to Umai shows, and remnants of their lan-

[ 177 ]

guage, which sounds like Yurok but whose meaning is partly lost, come into occasional ritual use, and Wogè words sometimes are given to a doctor to speak when in trance, but are not remembered by her afterward.

And what of the Yurok world? You might say it is the Greek concept of the *oikoumenê*, the habitable world, carried to an extreme. It is flat, and of a size which can be viewed from end to end, and traversed by a man in a canoe, or by a woman for that matter. (See diagrammatic end-paper map.) At its top is an upriver ocean, at its bottom a downriver ocean, while between the two flows the Klamath River, the center of the world being on the river, about halfway between top and bottom. It is a neat world, whose outermost boundaries are fixed, as well as each part within. And within is all that matters.

Now this world view is merely a Yurok sharpening of a similar pattern prevailing in most of California. My point is, (1) that it is immensely sharpened and (2) that without exegesis one feels at home in a Yurok story. It accomplishes the willing suspension of disbelief on its own merits.

The mood of "Umai" is a communicating one, with an aura of faint melancholy, as stories which take one very far back or very far forward in time seem always to have; it is a poetic expression of a state of newness and loneliness and emptiness in the world; it is about two girls, literally a world apart, their brief meeting and their parting, and about the glow from the sunset sky which unites them. It is simple and unremarkable and pleasing, and believable as is a story by Hans Christian Andersen. How far and with what ease its effortless form leads us, non-Yuroks, into an imagist acceptance of Yurok cosmogony, physiography, and world view!

[ 178 ]

As to its literary form, "Umai" is surely an idyll, fulfilling with elegance the dictionary definition as, "A poem or prose composition consisting of a 'little picture,' usually describing pastoral scenes or events or any charmingly simple episode."

## 7.  ABOUT-THE-HOUSE GIRL

IT is the Karok who tell the story, "About-the-House Girl." The Karok world begins where the Yurok world ends at Bluff Creek on the Klamath River, and extends upriver as far as Happy Camp close to the Oregon border. Still farther inland and belonging to yet another people (and world) are the Klamath Lakes, the source for the river, and in reality the Upriver Ocean of both Yurok and Karok geography.

The story has never been published, and my source is manuscript copy from the field notebooks of A. L. Kroeber, who recorded it in the early 1900's. For this and other stories and linguistic material, Mr. Kroeber had a talented trio of informants and storytellers, Little Ike, as he was called in English, Little Ike's wife, and his mother.

The Karok and Yurok are much alike physically, and in their way of life and world view, and in their superb story style. This latter common trait is of particular interest in the face of the total unlikeness of their languages, the Karok belonging to the *Hokan* linguistic stock, while the Yurok are presumably of remote *Algonquin* affiliation.

"About-the-House Girl" begins, progresses to its climax, and comes to an end with a sort of chekhovian elegance. The characterizations, motivations, and feelings as set forth in the

[ 179 ]

original translation are completely meaningful to one who knows nothing of the Karok world: not so, the events and their course. The Yurok and Karok presuppositions as to values, and their time and space sense, are so exotic to us and indeed to most Indians of other tribes, that much which is implicit in the story has to be somewhat elaborated and made explicit in the telling to a foreign audience. This is what I have tried to do, and it is all I have tried to do.

Just how very good were the trio of storytellers was brought home to me, not so much with "About-the-House Girl," which I was inclined to take for granted, as with the story of "Loon Woman." The Karok had picked up only a floating remnant of that story and had not troubled to elaborate on it, but it was the sense they made of that single bit which gave me a lead into the heart of the story as told elsewhere.

As to "About-the-House Girl," it is quite simply a love story, a romance having to do with a young man and a young woman, who meet, fall in love, and, in very truth, live happily ever after. See how closely it follows the romance pattern.

Both young people are virginal, pure, without sex experience. Each is at the far end of adolescence, ready to exchange his inexperience for adulthood, but introverted and shy, caught in a world of dreams and semi-reality.

The young man, Patapir (*Patapirihak* in Karok), sits by the river dreaming and playing his flute. He spends long hours in penance and prayer in the Karok way of course, which means he cuts and gathers wood according to set rules, makes a fire in the sacred house, the sweat house, where he sweats himself and prays, after which he dives naked into ocean or river. Across the river he sees two girls who are probably no better than they should be. Quaintly, he asks leave to make love to the two of them. They tease and evade him. But, meanwhile, like Romeo, Patapir glimpses Ifapi, his Juliet.

Ifapi (*Ivharak ifapi* in Karok) also approaches adulthood obliquely and by way of religion. There is a Leader of the Sacred Dances, overseas. Him she serves, hiding from the world except in her special role of priestess to the Leader, pretending otherwise to be sick, and keeping herself apart.

Patapir and Ifapi meet, and although it seems an altogether unremarkable meeting, they are in love from that time. Their mutual shyness is shed as though it had never been; consummation of their love comes soon.

There is even the romantic touch of Ifapi's father's disappointment when his daughter first tells him that she is married. He had hoped she would marry the flute player. There is his pleasure when he learns that it is indeed the flute player who is her husband. It is not so said, but there is a suspicion of implied meaning that Ifapi may well have shared this wish of her father's before Patapir first saw her in her disguise of sickness. It may have been for him that she was keeping herself apart.

And, whereas Ifapi's father joins the young people in their canoe voyage into the ocean world and beyond, Patapir's parents take their son's seemingly lighthearted removal from home with understandable sadness.

Straight romance as it is, the story is so saturated with the specifically Karok-Yurok world view that its most innocent seeming phrases lead straight into an ethnological treatise unless one restrains the impulse to explain such matters as, "Patapir's hair was very long, but he never knew girls," or, "Looking up to the house there, he saw an old woman on top, drying seaweed on the roof," or the *ten boats* of men setting

[ 181 ]

out to cross the ocean for an evening's lark, or the *Deerskin Dance,* or the *shame* the two girls feel upon learning that Patapir and Ifapi are married, their vanishing, and their leaving behind them "the little round basket hats" always worn by women in public, and frequently in the house too, or the "other side of the ocean."

The swings and changes of feeling and mood are kept within limits proper to an overall tone which is deeply felt, but contained. Its comic moments and its moments of sadness are not permitted to take over, there being a Mozartian upper and lower limit of allowed emotional expression. There is proportion and clarity. It is a formed story style, that of a grave romance.

## 8. TESILYA, SUN'S DAUGHTER

It was while rereading the full, leisurely narrative "Cane" from which "Tesilya, Sun's Daughter" is taken, that I first realized that the women of the native literature were not the faceless, generic female, but rather characterized individuals, and that if I looked I might even find a heroine.

There could be no less promising a place to look for my heroine than in "Cane." For with "Cane" we come to the literary form peculiar to the Mohave and other Yuman peoples of the lower Colorado River, a lengthy and elaborated narrative form, told for people who know well their considerable territory and who never tire of description of an infinity of exactly located geographic points of reference for the wanderings, wars, and amorous adventures of their heroes. Their tales are special in another way—each place, each episode, is set apart by a song or songs sung to celebrate and commemorate it; the prose narrative thus becomes epic-like in its style and formality with episodes strung between beads of song, and somehow suggesting the sort of material which could have been awaiting a Mohave Homer for transformation into poetry and true epic.

There is the further peculiarity in Mohave-Yuman narrative that the stories and songs are first dreamed, and it is the dreamer who then sings and tells his dream, and in this way his listeners learn the songs and at least parts of the narrative. Other peoples have visions or dreams that endow the dreamer with particular mystic knowledge and power. It is reserved to these Colorado River peoples to dream their entire literary *corpus*. To them, dreaming is moving back in time and in understanding to the beginnings of things when gods walked the new earth. They participate in the events and feelings and beliefs of those days by way of the dream, so that even the creation of the world may become part of the dreamer's own experience. This psychic projection into the ancestral and tribal past may occur at any time in life, but the significant dream experience will probably have come in the prenatal state, and it will be only after birth and years of growing that, gradually, the whole of the dream will be recovered; it may not be told in its entirety until late in life.

We may define the act of dreaming differently; but what the Mohave understand it to be does indeed influence their literature, which is almost surrealistically detailed and static in certain of its aspects, and dreamily shifting and changing in others. It is possible—it has been done—to pinpoint on a modern geodetic survey map of the Colorado River area of Cali-

fornia and Arizona the villages, the scenes of wars, the mountains, the passes, the springs, and the desert washes which are
named and described in such a dreamed myth, even to tracing
in detail the routes of long migrations made in mythical times.

This accuracy, this lingering and savoring of place and
event in story is, of course, something the Mohave like to do
today next best to actually travelling to familiar but distant
places within their own land (or having a war on the good
old pattern, which is no longer allowed). In these preferences
and habits they are unlike most other California Indians—
just as their stories are unlike others. The Mohave, as far back
as their or our knowledge goes, lived on the river. Each year
the river brought its deposit of rich, red silt at floodtime.
When the flood receded, the Mohave planted his corn, his
squash and beans. The rains and the sun saw to the growing
of his crop. The river carried a full catch of fish, and the fruit
of the mesquite tree which grows above the flood line was
abundant and his for the gathering. He lived on a larger land,
with more economic leeway than most California Indians. He
and his wife and his children were for the most part sturdy,
well fed and well housed, and his old folks were cared for.
And still there was leisure for the manly sport of war—
close-up in-fighting with heavy wooden clubs—and for travelling. He followed both avocations with gusto and recalled
them afterward with satisfaction.

A Mohave woman had equal rights with men. She owned
property, she did not marry against her wish, she was given a
divorce for the asking. She was, generally speaking, strong
and self-respecting and open. She and the children and old
people by preference confined their travelling to friendly villages well within their own territory, and she did not engage

in war. She hated it, regarding it as dangerous and potentially disastrous: somebody's head got broken in those close-up clubbing contests, and someday it might be one's own husband. It was one of the vagaries of men to be put up with.

It is men who dream the dreams of song and story—we know very little about women's dreaming. By their own report they rarely dream. The women who come into the dreams of the men are indubitably Mohave women in behavior, looks, dress; but as to their names, age, status, and where they lived, these are the dreamily shifting matters not by any means to be pinned down. A reading of "Cane" gives a vivid and consistent picture of the woman who was the hero's wife and the mother of his hero son. But she will one time be called Tesilya (Mohave, *Tšese'ilye*), another time Tesilya's daughter. She will be Sun's daughter; she will also be referred to as Sun's wife. Sometimes she comes from the north, not the east. Or she is two women, two wives. What nonetheless is clear is the characterization and the consistent feeling-tone of the narrator of the dream toward her. So, by whatever name Bluebird, the narrator of "Cane," called her, I use the name he gave her most often and tell her story according to his portrayal as I understand it.

Tesilya's is the only story of the nine which is a fragment of the whole. The episodes in which she figures are themselves separated by songs and lengthy narrative. I lifted them out in the order of their occurrence and, as it were, pushed them together, closing the gaps between, and making one Tesilya of the dream-varied woman or women. Because of the fragmentation and the lifting from context, I included her story only after long hesitation. In the end, I could not leave her out.

Tesilya is a lovely lady, and her story exemplifies what can sometimes be the reward of reading folklore as literature.

For the Mohave Indians, the story "Cane" refreshes their knowledge of two of their ancient heroes, of the murder of one and its revenge by the other, of the heroes' loves and their wanderings. Formal framing is accomplished by the cosmological disposition of its principal actors at the end of the story, which is studded and decorated with songs. It never centers on a woman, or so the Mohave would say. But some of its most poignant scenes have a woman at their center, and some of the acts of high courage are performed by women. It is a richly endowed story style with a spill-over of qualities and values beyond those its hearers are consciously attuned to hear in it: its women are as vivid as its wars. A single phrase or sentence will often tell a great deal about a woman: "She took a white peeled willow stick, *qara'asap,* to sweep the dress under her thighs so as not to crumple it when she sat down." Here is another: "Now the three men felt glad, when they saw her grinding corn. They looked to see how she worked; all of them smiled. 'See how beautiful she looks,' they said. She was clean and wore beads around her neck and on her ears and wrists, and a dress of willow bark, and was painted."

The Mohave story style is prose epic in temper and tempo. The subject matter is of gods and heroes and their enemies. There are love episodes, but these are subordinate to the heroic theme. A hero is born a hero and his actions are worthy actions appropriate to a hero. His enemies use supernatural power for unworthy ends, and are ultimately overcome by the superior supernatural power of the hero. Each character is defined, consistent, vivid, believable within the epic frame. The women and occasional minor characters such as the old uncle in "Cane" would at times be equally believable in a romantic or even a naturalistic frame.

But Tesilya and the other women of their dreams suit the classic epic role well. They are fit wives and mothers of heroes: they are beautiful, they are classically poised and sufficiently complaisant. The role of wicked temptress, of tragic wife or mother, which we find in Greek epic, is not prefigured in the Mohave vision, perhaps because with them women do not go in much for magic, thereby escaping, anciently and in myth as in real life, the heavy burdens and heady power of magic and control of the supernatural.

Tesilya is as much a heroine as the epic-tending form in which she comes to us allows. I cannot greatly blame Bluebird's frequent multiplying of her to more than one.

If you are ever on the Colorado River in the region of its great valley, you will see Mohave women from time to time who will remind you of Tesilya. You will recognize the repose, the beauty, and the reserves of strength, and in imagination you will see one or another of these women setting off, undaunted and alone, toward Sun's house.

## 9. THE MAN'S WIFE

"THE Man's Wife" is a poetic, gentle, and ultimately tragic story born of the human refusal to accept the death of a beloved one as a final and irrevocable separation. The theme is, I suppose, as old as man. All religious creeds take a position regarding immortality. One creed may be positive, personal, and specific, saying that I, my personality and appearance intact, shall find after death my mother and father, my wife and son and daughter and friend, unchanged. Another may be mystic, teaching that the essence of the personality is indestructible and separable from the destructible body. Or there is the negative, non-personal view, teaching that the individual is absorbed into an undifferentiated whole without consciousness or identity, but somehow viable, and hence comforting.

Ever since man has stood securely on two feet and raised his hands and eyes freely to the sun, there have been individuals who have accepted the limited span whatever their role, whatever love and pain it brought, as their personal beginning and end. They neither cry for more nor believe that there is more than the life two hands can hold and perhaps mold, changing the world by this much from what it was before they lived. But these are the rare ones. A codified system of belief which asks of a whole people that it renounce its mystic, prelogical yearning for some sort of afterlife is doomed, and it soon becomes reduced to a secular vulgarity, its dogma of unbelief intolerant, the will to power emerging as the only adequate anodyne to belief.

So, for most peoples, there is a land of the dead whose direction and approximate location are known. And tales are told of what happens when a bereaved person determines on going to that land and bringing back his beloved. Sometimes he succeeds. Our Indians, who played many variations on the theme, tell of an occasional recovery from seeming death with return to the world of the living. And the Japanese have some remarkably attractive ghost wives amongst the living in their stories, who are, however, vulnerable to discovery and other hazards special to their state.

Usually the effort to bring back one who has died is not successful. Most people sympathize with the wish to do so, but the actuality runs into almost insuperable ambiguities and ambivalences: the widespread dread of the presence of the dead; the awareness of the corruptible body; the potential danger to the living in the indestructible essence which one cannot see or in any way control. Then there is the sense of propriety. Alive, one dwells here and does thus and so. Dead, one dwells elsewhere and follows another thus and so. There is the reasonable reluctance to go against the will of the gods, and a suspicion and fear of him who defies them. There is, after all, a way, an order in life which must be observed, else no one knows what may happen.

It is no wonder the theme has engaged the makers and tellers of stories, with its variety of emotional overtones, its equivocation and conflict.

My sources for "A Man's Wife," a story of a husband's effort to recover his dead wife, are the eleven versions which Dr. Ann Gayton collected and published from the Yokuts and Western Mono Indians, whose homeland is the San Joaquin Valley in the region of Tulare Lake and eastward to the watershed of the Sierra Nevada Mountains. The story is stable in its principal parts, which are as well known as the series of episodes for "Pandora's Box," or for "Bellerophon." Some versions are fuller than others, and there are some preferential differences as to ending, but anyone competent to tell a story at all could tell this one adequately.

Perhaps the Yokuts have a special feeling for the theme. In any case, they use the elements one has come to associate with the Orpheus story without forcing too much distracting action, and—except for an occasional false note resulting from the addition of a motivation or an action belonging to another story or in another context—they use them without too much heightening of emotion, and without blurring the feeling and meaning with extraneous events or emotions. Their story retains for the most part a simplicity and a benevolence which is the ideal "mean" for the subject matter.

I am conscious of very little native conceptualization of a sort to trouble a non-Indian. That the land of the dead should lie toward the west with a trail leading there for the dead to follow, that the dead should be visible only after sundown, that they should play games and dance, and that they should find the odor of the living disagreeable are concepts accessible to anyone. Also, that there should be a chief of the land of the dead, and that he should make certain conditions before allowing the man to take his wife away with him are elements familiar from the Greek story. Orpheus made the descent into Tartarus to try to recover Eurydice, his wife; with his music he charmed Charon, Cerberus, the judges, and Hades himself. He was allowed to take Eurydice back with him, the condition Hades made being that Orpheus must not look back until his wife was again in the sunlight. Orpheus turned back to look at her too soon, and so lost her forever.

The correspondences between the Greek story and the Yokuts are not specific, and the seeming similarity lies perhaps in the limits of the human imagination. Given a plot so circumscribed, not too wide a variety can be expected in its solution. Even the episode of Eurydice meeting death in a serpent's sting has no specific equivalent in the Yokuts' story, although in the coda which some of the versions include, the man ultimately dies from a snake bite. But this is a motif that Indians and Greeks have used in other stories and connotations. The adder of Thrace and the rattlesnake of western North America are very different, and would presumably be used with different meanings and significances.

Reading the Greek and Yokuts stories, who is to call whom primitive? The raw material from which are spun the tales that live to be told and retold to children and grandchildren is usually primitive in that it is the concretization of something arising from the unconscious: a love, a hate, a longing, a fear, a question. And if the tale is so well spun that the love is realized, the hate avenged or dispersed, the longing assuaged, the fear generalized and shared, or the question answered, then the author, the teller, and the audience, whether Yokuts or Greek or modern American, are functioning on a level not primitive nor necessarily sophisticated, but wholly human, which functioning I take to be an early aspect of art.

# Sources

Curtin, Jeremiah. *Creation Myths of Primitive America*. Boston, 1898.

——, *Myths of the Modocs*. Boston, 1912.

Demetracopoulou, Dorothy. "The Loon Woman Myth: A Study in Synthesis." *Journal of American Folklore*, v. 46, 1933.

Dixon, Roland B. "Achomawi and Atsugewi Tales." *Journal of American Folklore*, v. 21, 1908. Dixon's No. 5, "Loon Woman" (Achomawi) and No. 12, "Flint Man, The Search for Fire, and Loon Woman" (Atsugewi) are sources for my story No. 2, "Loon Woman."

——, "Maidu Myths." *Bulletin of the American Museum of Natural History* (New York), v. 17, 1902. Dixon's No. 7, "The Loon Woman," is a source for my No. 2, "The Loon Woman." Dixon's No. 12, "The Tolowim-Woman and the Butterfly Man," is the source story for my No. 3, "Butterfly Man."

——, "Shasta Myths." *Journal of American Folklore*, v. 23, 1910. Dixon's No. 4, "The Girl Who Married Her Brother," is one source for my No. 2, "Loon Woman."

DuBois, Cora. "Wintu Ethnography." *Univ. of Calif. Publs. in American Archaeology and Ethnology,* v. 36, 1935.

DuBois, Cora, and Dorothy Demetracopoulou. "Wintu Myths." *Univ. of Calif. Publs. in American Archaeology and Ethnology,* v. 28, 1931. No. 5, "Loknorharas," is the source story for my No. 4, "Dance Mad;" and No. 37, "Talimleluheres and Loon Woman," and No. 38, "Talimleluheres and Rolling Head and Loon Woman," are two of the sources for my No. 2, "Loon Woman."

Farrand, Livingston. "Shasta and Athapascan Myths from Oregon." Leo J. Frachtenberg, ed. *Journal of American Folklore,* v. 28, 1915. Farrand's No. 5, "The Girl Who Married Her Brother," is a source for my No. 2, "Loon Woman."

Gayton, Anna H. "The Orpheus Myth in North America." *Journal of American Folklore,* v. 48, 1935.

———, and Stanley S. Newman. "Yokuts and Western Mono Myths." *Univ. of California Anthropological Records,* v. 5, 1940. Gayton's 3, 4, 6, 16, 17, 25, 34, 54, and 55 are different versions of "Pursuit of a Dead Wife" and principal sources for my No. 9, "The Man's Wife." Nos. 139-153 are "abstracts" of same with "comparative notes."

Gifford, Edward Winslow. "Western Mono Myths." *Journal of American Folklore,* v. 36, 1923. Gifford's No. 12, "A Visit to the World of the Dead," is a source for my No. 9, "A Man's Wife."

Kroeber, A. L. *Handbook of the Indians of California.* Smithsonian Institution of Washington, D.C., Bureau of American Ethnology, Bulletin 78, 1925.

———, "Indian Myths of South Central California." *Univ. of Calif. Publs. in American Archaeology and Ethnology,* v. 4, 1907. Kroeber's No. 24, "The Visit to the Dead," and No. 35, same title, are two sources for my No. 9, "The Man's Wife."

———, "Seven Mohave Myths." *Univ. of Calif. Anthropological Records,* v. 11, no. 1, 1948. Kroeber's No. 1, "Cane," is the source for my No. 8, "Tesilya, Sun's Daughter."

———, "Loon Woman." Typewritten copy from field notebook of Karok myths. Unpublished. It is one source for my No. 2, "Loon Woman."

———, "Across-Ocean-Dance." Typewritten copy from field notebook of Karok myths. Unpublished. It is the source for my No. 7, "About-the-House Girl."

Merriam, C. Hart. *An-Nik-A-Del.* Boston, 1928.

Sapir, Edward. "Yana Texts." *Univ. of Calif. Publs. in American Archaeology and Ethnology,* v. 9, 1910. Sapir's No. 10, "Coyote, Pine-Martin, and Loon," and No. 12 (of the supplement, "Yana Myths Collected by Roland B. Dixon") are two sources for my No. 2, "Loon Woman." No. 20, "Spell Said by a Girl Desirous of Getting a Husband," is the source for my "Love Charm," No. 5.

Spott, Robert, and A. L. Kroeber. "Yurok Narratives." *Univ. of Calif. Publs. in American Archaeology and Ethnology,* v. 35, 1942. Their No. 24, "The Inland Whale," is the printed source for my No. 1, "The Inland Whale." Their No. 37, "Upriver Ocean Girl," is the source for my No. 6, "Umai."

Waterman, Thomas T. "Yurok Geography." *Univ. of Calif. Publs. in American Archaeology and Ethnology,* v. 16, 1920.